Always Smiling

Always Smiling

GEORGIA TOFFOLO

Quercus

First published in Great Britain in 2018 by

Quercus Editions Ltd
Carmelite House
50 Victoria Embankment
London EC4Y 0DZ

An Hachette UK company

A CIP catalogue record for this book is available
from the British Library

HB ISBN 978 1 78747 504 5
TPB ISBN 978 1 78747 579 3

All photographs supplied by the author.

10 9 8 7 6 5 4 3 2 1

Text designed and typeset by CC Book Production

Printed and bound in Great Britain by Clays Ltd, Elcograf S.p.A.

I dedicate this book to my grandparents.
I love you both.

Contents

Introduction

Honestly, I was *convinced* that I would be one of the first people voted out of the jungle. That was why I thought I kept having to do all of the challenges. I was convinced that everyone saw me as a silly posh girl, and they just wanted to watch me making a prat of myself. To be fair, I felt a bit like a silly posh girl. I never felt as though I was especially brave – or that knowing my way up and down the King's Road would prepare me for picking up snakes in the bush. Let me put it this way: kangaroo anus is *not* on the menu at the Bluebird!

However, my time in the jungle made me realize that it really doesn't matter where you come from, or what you're used to. You just need to remember your best life lessons and be prepared to keep learning. All that counts is that you keep smiling, and remember to try your hardest. Sometimes, you go through things that are frightening in an obvious way, a way that's easy for everyone to understand – like being trapped in a tank and covered with the sort of spiders that are so enormous, they seem to have knees and elbows. (I don't believe for a second that they're more scared of us than we are of them. Spiders like human flesh, and they do *not* do Veganuary.) Yet, sometimes life is terrifying in a way that affects your brain as much as your body, and emotional challenges can be just as difficult to deal with as physical ones. In so many ways, I'm incredibly lucky. My family are crazily loving, and, let's be real, sometimes plain crazy – but they've always kept me grounded. They make sure that I'm always 'up', but they will never, ever let me be up myself. It's thanks to them that I discovered I had secret strengths during my time in Australia, because they've always made me believe that I could do anything, if I tried hard enough. They also know how to tease me when my feet need to touch the ground.

Anyone who knows me well, realizes I have more than my fair share of energy. And anyone who has just met me will wonder whether I've got secret cans of Red Bull stashed in my socks. It takes a lot to bring me down, and I have a tendency to leap out of bed grinning and yelling, 'Good morning, world!' Although, I'll admit that there have been occasions when things got out of hand the night before, I've slept through my alarm, and a 'Good afternoon, world' would be much more appropriate.

Even though I'm cheerful by nature, sometimes I struggle with insecurity and self-doubt, because it's hard to be a woman in the world. I'm a proud feminist, and I think that life is becoming so much better for all of us, and more inspiring women than ever are standing up and speaking out. But, every day, I'm dealing with the same problems that we all face. Sometimes, it's being furious about the news and the way some people still seem so backwards when we talk about women's rights. Sometimes, it's because I'm angry about creepy guys being sexist and horrible to my girlfriends. And I'm embarrassed to admit this, but sometimes it's posting a selfie on Instagram, deciding I hate it and then obsessing over the one person who left a mean comment under the picture. I've been on the T.V. show *Made in Chelsea* since I was just under nineteen, and I don't think I'll ever get used to the way it feels to have millions of strangers comment on my face and body, even when they're saying nice things. The weird thing is, most of my friends aren't on T.V., but they still have the same insecurities and anxieties. Social media can be brilliant, but it's tough for all of us to grow up in a world where we feel as though other people's opinions matter so much. In my book, I want to talk about how it's OK to find this difficult, and how we can work out a way of having fun with selfies, and making sure they don't make us sad.

One thing that always makes me feel good about myself is

> ❛ My family are crazily loving, and, let's be real, sometimes plain crazy – but they've always kept me grounded. ❜

having fun with fashion! So many people make fun of Chelsea girls, and claim that we spend our lives going to the shops. Firstly, this is a lie. We spend our lives on the Internet, ordering things from the shops! After that, we spend the rest of our time feeling slightly guilty as they all pile up on the bedroom floor, and we wonder when we'll ever get a chance to go to the Post Office and send them back. That reminds me, I must Google my nearest Post Office ... Seriously, though, there's nothing silly or frivolous about wanting to look good, and over the last few years, I've discovered that putting together the right outfits makes me feel incredibly confident, and ready for anything. I have to be. While I love feeling comfy and cosy, my friends have a tendency to plan parties with the strangest, most specific themes. I spend a lot of time standing in front of my wardrobe and wondering whether I've got anything that screams 'Versailles' or '1960s Manhattan' or 'Roaring Twenties Royalty'. Then there's my job at *The Lady*, where I need to look office appropriate and simultaneously stylish, timeless and, er, ladylike. I mean, you never know when you'll be sent out to meet the Queen. It hasn't happened yet, but I'm stockpiling the cashmere. It could be any day now! Ultimately, I think I'm a bit of a style chameleon, and it's one of the things I love the most about being in my twenties. We don't have to dress to define our identities, but we can use fashion to celebrate, to explore new aspects of our personalities and to find out what really makes us feel good. It's not just about what fits our bodies, but finding clothes to fit our moods, too. I'm going to be sharing my tips for occasion dressing, and I'll be covering the most serious and silly occasions I can think of. I'll also be talking about how we can all find our personal style, and why the best way to hit the shops (or Internet shops) is with a big smile on your face.

Now, if you've ever seen an episode of *Made in Chelsea*, you'll know that parties are a big part of my life. The best thing about being young and living in London is that you never, ever run out of opportunities to have fun. However, I think that partying is a way of life that can be embraced no matter where you are. I firmly believe that if I lived in a hamlet in the Outer Hebrides, and I could only reach my nearest neighbour by canoe, I'd find a way to get the party started. At the moment, I think that life can feel very serious and scary for many of us. In many ways, it doesn't feel like the perfect time to party – but that's why this is the best time to do it. We need fun more than ever. There's a time and a place to focus on our worries and concerns, but we need to relax and give ourselves some time and space to be completely carefree, too. Now, some people like to do this on top of a mountain, listening to chanting monks and carving their own wind chimes out of bird poo. I like to do this by opening a bottle of champagne, kicking my shoes off and leaping on to the nearest table so that I can showcase my best moves. Both methods work, but if you're worried that you've forgotten how to truly kick back, you can learn from my party philosophy. Jägerbombs are optional, FUN is mandatory.

Because, after all, it doesn't really matter how much we achieve if we're not having fun, too. I think I'm really ambitious, and that's one of the parts of being a twenty-first-century woman that I love

Our lives are filled with challenges, but there are also ∪nities, as long as we know where to look for them and we're ∠pared to make them happen, too. But we need to be ambitious for ourselves, not to please our parents or impress our friends. Whenever I've made a bad decision, whether it's about a job, a friend, or romance, I've made it because I wasn't doing it for me. I make mistakes when I'm trying to impress the wrong people, or hoping to convince everyone that I'm happy doing what I *should* be doing, instead of what I *want* to be doing. Weirdly, the less I care about what people think of me, the more successful I feel. I think it's because the best way to be happy is to set your own rules. My best rule is that being kind is more important than being cool. Trying to behave in a way that impresses other people has always held me back, and I've spent the first part of my twenties discovering that I don't need to impress anyone but myself. The people who know us best don't care about the number of 'likes' we get, who we're working with, or who we're dating. They just want us to be happy, and they'll celebrate us when we're feeling proud, and look after us when we're going through difficult patches. Once we've learned that we don't need to achieve for anyone but ourselves, we can do anything. Our goals and dreams don't have any limit, apart from our own imaginations!

My best friends mean everything to me, but I've discovered that friendship can be just as challenging, scary and intense as any romantic relationship. One of the things I love the most about my life is that I have the chance to meet people from everywhere, and I've forged friendships that exist far outside the Chelsea bubble, as well as staying close with old pals who remember that embarrassing day when I wet myself in assembly. Stop laughing! It's the sort of thing that could happen to any seventeen-year-old! Seriously, I adore the fact that I have so many fabulous friends, from every era of my life, and I suspect I'll spend the rest of my life making new ones. Still, friendship isn't always an easy journey, and I've definitely discovered that some people are supposed to be in your life forever, and others aren't supposed to be in your life at all. I'll be exploring how to assemble your ultimate squad, how to recover when friendship goes wrong, and I'll be looking at just what makes friendship so magical when it works. One of my favourite recent discoveries about friendship is that it defies generations. Some of my best friends are going through experiences that are very similar to my own, but I've become friends with people who are much older and wiser than I am, and I feel so lucky to have the chance to learn from them. The best thing about intergenerational friendship is that proper adults know how to worry less. These are the people who call me out when I'm obsessing about who hasn't replied to my WhatsApp, or what I should do about leaving my phone and favourite jacket in an Uber . . .

Which brings us on to adulting! Whether you are utterly appalled by the fact that we've had to make up a brand-new verb, which just means 'getting on with things', or whether you just Instagrammed your gas bill with an *#adulting* tag, you can't deny that being a grown-up isn't always the easiest thing in the world. As a twenty-three-year-old, I know that I still have tons to learn – but, at the same time, in some ways, the last three years have been more educational than my entire A-level syllabus! On that theme, there are some serious subjects I'd like to share. I studied Politics at the University of Westminster, a subject I'm deeply passionate about, but I dropped out of the course! It took so much soul searching when it came to deciding that it wasn't the right place for me to be, but leaving university might be one of the most grown-up things I've ever done. It was so much scarier than walking the plank, or meeting a thousand snakes. Seriously, I would hold a snake a day rather than go through that experience again. I'd sleep with a snake in my bed. I'd *date* a snake. (Actually, I suppose I did that a while ago, and his name began with an *S*, too . . . More on that later.) Still, we're told that winners never quit, and quitters never win. No one ever explains that quitting is sometimes the most positive, liberating, healthy move to make. I'm going to be talking about finding the courage to quit, how we can learn to trust our instincts, and why, sometimes, the only advice worth taking is your own.

> The best way to be happy is to set your own rules.

Going back to the subject of snakes for a second, I think we need to talk about romance. I've been in love. I've had my heart broken. I've felt vulnerable in relationships, I've pursued people who've hurt me and I've stood up for myself and learned not to let anyone take me for granted. Ultimately, I'm still a romantic. I believe in love, and that it takes a while to find the One. Still, it's OK, as long as you have lots of fun finding them. Since I started dating, I've been getting to know myself and working out the difference between Mr Right and Mr Wrong. To quote the most stylish romantic heroine of all time, Cher Horowitz from *Clueless*: 'You know how fussy I am about my shoes, and they only go on my feet.' I believe girls everywhere need to be much, much choosier! I want to talk about why it's so important for us all to be serious about dating, simply because we can only be with the people who are prepared to take us seriously and treat us with respect.

In Chelsea, I see a lot of bad behaviour and double standards. Guys think it's OK to play around, but girls are judged for doing exactly the same thing. As far as I'm concerned, it doesn't matter what you do or who you do it with, as long as you don't lie and don't hurt anyone. I want to talk about the importance of self-respect when it comes to love and dating. We attract people who see us the way we see ourselves, so, as long as we're happy in ourselves, we'll meet the people who will be good to us. Also, let's be real: being single is *the most fun*. Sometimes, nothing could be nicer than curling up with a cute boy and *The Notebook*, with your phone on airplane and hidden in a different room. And, sometimes, all we want to do is lead a conga line down the Fulham Road and keep going until we bump into the milkman. Falling in love is wonderful, but it's so much better to be alone and loving life than feeling insecure because you're with someone who doesn't love you. I also have tons of extremely helpful, practical advice about finding first-date locations where you definitely won't bump into your ex, and being aware of any romantic red flags. If you like someone and he offers to show you his robots, *run*.

Ultimately, I know that most of the people who want to share life advice are slightly more mature in years than I am. I'm still in my early twenties, and I feel as though I learn a new life lesson every day. However, I'm fortunate enough to have seen and experienced things that I never thought I'd get to try, and every single moment has made me wiser and even more determined to get the most out of every new adventure. Admittedly, I might not have the philosophical wisdom of Proust, or the worldly, hard-won wit of Dorothy Parker, but I *promise* you that no one else knows as much as I do about getting glitter out of your hair. Every single thing that happens to us has a funny side. There will always be a party to go to, a new friend to meet, a trip, a joke or the chance to speak up and make a difference. Speaking up for what I believe in is so important to me, but I also care about making tiny differences. Every day, we have the chance to smile, say yes, and make an impact on other people's lives. We don't have to go all the way to the jungle for our words and actions to travel for millions of miles; let's make them happy, positive ones.

Love,

Toff

Friendship

My friends truly mean absolutely everything to me. They're my London family, and we all know that someone doesn't need to be a blood relation in order to be extremely close to you. My world is made up of surrogate sisters, brothers from other mothers, pretend parents and honorary aunties. However, we also know that friendship can be about eight thousand times more complicated than any romantic relationship or love affair. A friend can make your day or break your heart. Best friends are for life, but bad friends will ruin your life. Some of my friends have made me skip down the street, singing, and some of my friends have made me cry. Having said all that, I can put my hand on my heart and say there is nothing I would change about my friendships. The people I have chosen to have in my life are the ones who have helped me to discover who I am. Even painful friendships can be transformative and teach you all kinds of lessons. I truly believe that the older we get, the better we become at friendship, which is an inspiring thing to remember. If you're having a rubbish time and you're hoping that your friendship situation will improve, time will probably make everything better.

I'm in a slightly strange situation, because anyone who wants to watch how my friendships work can see it on a screen. *Made in Chelsea* is driven by group dynamics, and it's natural for us to separate off into little tribes. However, my life gets quite complicated because so many of my friends belong to separate tribes, so this means that I'm often caught between several sets of drama! This can be incredibly stressful; I really am a bit of a hippy – albeit one with an addiction to heated rollers – and I just want everyone to get along. However, when I got to the jungle, I couldn't believe how useful my diplomatic skills could be! I've spent years working out how to diffuse tension, stop screaming matches and take the edge off everyone's biggest outbursts. To my surprise, these skills were much more useful than, say, a diploma in bug cookery or a year at snake school. That's not to say that being a good friend to people is about keeping the peace at any cost. I'm outspoken, I love to debate and I have some strong opinions that I'm keen to share – but I've always thought that being right all the time is much less important than being a good friend, which definitely helped during some of the especially tense moments in the jungle!

If you want to be my friend, you only really need two qualifications: you must be kind and you must be good fun. I don't think

I could be close to anyone who didn't make me laugh or anyone who didn't remember to get their round in. A good friend needs to be kind, loving, cheering and supportive, but also unafraid to tell you when you're being a bit of a shit. When it comes to friendship, a little tough love goes a long way. A lot is just meanness. Friends are the ones who encourage you to dream, while making sure you stay real enough to function.

What it's like to work with your friends

The odd thing about *Made in Chelsea* is that it's extremely incestuous, friendship-wise. Everyone is a mate of a mate. What's weird about it is that most people don't work for companies that also employ their best friends!

Most of the time, working with my best friends is a total treat. I'm delighted that we can spend time together, going about our day and treating the Bluebird like our business premises. However, putting those friendships in the spotlight puts a lot of pressure on those relationships, and that can make things difficult in the long term. Two of my best friends, Emily and Jess, aren't in the show anymore, and I think that's been a really positive thing for us, because we can relax a bit more. Together, we're all much more funny and interesting when we're not worrying about being filmed and *looking* funny and interesting! However, being on the programme has led me to forge friendships with all sorts of new people that I truly adore. Mark, Victoria, Mimi and Mytton were completely new to me – and getting to know them has been a total joy, and an education, too! I think that new friends are one of the best things you can gain from any job. It's the bonus that just keeps getting bigger.

Even die-hard fans of *Made in Chelsea* don't always know quite how real a reality show actually is. I know plenty of people think everything is made up, but actually everything that takes place is really happening. This means that everything you see is real, but it also means that my life has had a distinctly unreal quality for the last four years!

I think the best thing *Made in Chelsea* has taught me is to be myself. It's so much easier to be relaxed on camera when you're used to being filmed doing nothing at all. I'm not worried about sounding like an idiot or not having anything serious to say, because I've never taken it too seriously and it's always worked out fine. Also, I think that most of us are living in our own reality shows. It doesn't matter whether or not we're actually on T.V. We're all choosing to document and share the highlights of our lives. The only difference is that, when I'm on television, I don't get to showcase my best bits – what goes out to the world is beyond my control. I think this has taught me to be much more relaxed. Everyone already knows I'm not perfect, so the pressure is off. People all over the world have seen me at my worst and most vulnerable, and that makes me feel strong because I don't have anything to be scared of. I'm not an actor, and I can't hide my feelings or pretend to be anything I'm not – but *Made in Chelsea* has taught me to be happy in my own skin, literally and figuratively.

How it feels to be betrayed by a friend

I hate to say it, but I wonder whether betrayal is an important part of growing up. At some point, I think we're all let down by people we trust, and it's impossibly painful. It's really difficult to get over it and heal; all you can do is wait. If nothing else, you learn so much about which friends will support you and be kind to you, and which ones just don't care. Who would stop to help you if you got knocked over in a queue for discount Chanel handbags, and who would tread on your broken body in order to buy the 2.55 that you've always dreamed of. Sadly, I found that out on the show when a burgeoning romance went wrong. Liv, a girl I'd always been friendly with, if not super close to, decided she wanted a summer fling with Francis, the boy I'd been seeing – and she made her move. I'm sorry, but, if you ask me, all is not fair in love and war. I would never do that to another woman, even if it was over a man who wasn't especially keen.

The worst part of the whole event was the humiliation, and that Liv thought that getting what she wanted was more important than making sure my feelings weren't hurt. If she and Francis were now married with a baby on the way, I might be able to admit that I should have stood aside – but I was made to feel utterly heartbroken and wobbly for months, all for the sake of their quick summer romance.

I know we're all capable of doing silly things on impulse, especially when we're young, and that it isn't fair to blame Liv entirely, when Francis was interested, or to blame Francis for not wanting to pursue things with me. But being hurt, especially in such a public way, has redefined what I look for in friends, and the way I see friendship. It's also made me understand and empathize with other people's vulnerabilities. But I need friends who will be understanding and compassionate when I'm feeling insecure – and, first and foremost, friends who would never put boys before our friendship. After all, boys are absolutely bloody everywhere. You can literally go to any bar in Chelsea and find a hot boy I've never met. Why would you go out of your way to *specifically* pursue the person I have feelings for?

To be fair, I suspect Francis downplayed everything that happened with me when he started seeing Liv. Maybe, at the time, Liv was sure that the relationship was going somewhere. The whole saga is filled with more feeling than a therapist's waiting room. Sometimes, it still makes me feel quite raw – and it seems as though I've lost two friends over it. However, I do think that this has made me a better friend. It's forced me to make sure that I treat people as I expect to be treated, and I don't lower my standards to make anyone's life easier. I know I'm entitled to the same levels of kindness, respect and decency that I bring to any of my relationships, and if people can't match those levels, I can't have them in my life. Also, I want to make sure that I'm never the sort of friend who makes other people insecure or unsure of themselves.

While the whole horrible drama destroyed a couple of my friendships, it made others so much stronger. It was so lovely to see how supportive everyone could be. If my friends hadn't been there to look after me and help me get through it, I honestly think that I might still be stuck in the South of France, crying on a yacht. The experience taught me that I must never take good friendships for granted. They are incredibly rare and precious. Also, that holiday romances might be the stuff of cheesy cliché, but holiday heartbreak is all too real. Next time I have my heart broken, I want to be back in Chelsea, close to work and all kinds of distractions that I can throw myself into. There is nothing fun about crying on a sun lounger. Still, it was one of the biggest learning experiences of my life and, when I look back on it, I remember the fun times too, and the way that the crisis brought out the best in my girls. Usually, I'm not a great believer in taking sides, but when one friend betrays you, it's comforting to discover that everyone you love is on your team.

Friends, old and new – why I love intergenerational friendships

One of the most positive lessons I have learned about paldom is that, when it comes to age and experience, there is absolutely no point limiting yourself. You can always find common ground with people, no matter what their age or background, and you can have a much more enriching, exciting friendship if those things are completely different from yours.

When I went into the jungle, the experience brought me a

brand-new best friend, Stanley. On the surface, we don't have much in common. His children are older than me. He thinks YouTube is called '*the* YouTube'. I'm not sure that he's ever been late in his life. Yet, he's one of my very favourite people to go to lunch with. Our friendship even has a Brangelina-style portmanteau: when we're together, we're Stoffley. In Stanley, I've finally found a friend who loves Winston Churchill as much as I do. I can't believe I had to go all the way to Australia to meet someone who is up for visiting the War Rooms with me.

The seven friends who will make your life heaven

We need friends. While we're drawn to people that we want to spend time with, and we make choices about the people who we want to have in our lives, friendship itself isn't optional, but essential. We need friendship to thrive. Our friends help us to make sense of who we are, what we want and where we're going. Above all, our friends are the people that we have fun with, and while we think of fun as an extra or a treat, we need that, too. It's not so much the cherry on top of the cake as the milk on your Cornflakes, or maybe a better example would be the avocado on your toast! One of the biggest life lessons I've learned in my twenties is that different friends cater for different emotional needs. In our teens, I think it's natural to have an intense 'best' friendship, but adulthood is all about the gathering of the clan. We all need a group of friends who can help us in different ways, at different times. Some of our friends will be quite sorted and sensible, and they are great at calming us down when we've missed a big deadline, or our bank card has just been swallowed by an A.T.M. However, we also need the naughty friends who will keep life interesting by suggesting that the best way to respond to a crisis is with a round of tequila. In fact, if it wasn't for the naughty friends,

> ' A good friend needs to be kind, loving, cheering and supportive, but also unafraid to tell you when you're being a bit of a shit. '

we wouldn't miss deadlines and lose cash cards, so they give the sensible friends a purpose. It's the circle of life!

Now, this might sound a little bit selfish and demanding, but it's worth remembering that your gossipy friend might be someone else's most grown-up friend, or that someone loves being your wisest pal, because you're the one who keeps leading them down the garden path and giving them the opportunity to make mischief. We are all different things to different people, and finding friends with different functions is just one way of spreading the love! We're all a bit like tiny companies, and we need to make sure there's someone on board who knows how to handle the accounts, and someone else who can plan the Christmas party. Here's a list of the different friends we all need in our lives, and why – and some of the people I love, who fulfil that function.

The Cheerleaders (Emily and Lottie)

I think that the most important friend a girl could have is someone who is genuinely pleased for her, who will wave metaphorical pompoms while screaming her name, and sometimes real ones, too.

As someone who spends a lot of time on social media, I have days when I feel as though everyone is out to put me down, and it doesn't matter how hard I work or how positive I try to be, it's a struggle to stay cheerful. Emily and Lottie are my Cheerleaders because they're positive about absolutely everything. If there's a horrible story in the paper about something mean that an ex said about me, Lottie will be the first to text with, *OMG, you look so hot in that photo!* And when something really exciting happens in my life, like getting the *This Morning* job, I know I can tell Emily without worrying that I'm showing off, and I don't need to play down my achievements. The trouble with modern life is that we feel as though we constantly have to be self-deprecating and ironic, and sometimes you do just want to scream, 'GO, ME! Everything is amazing!' without having someone tell you to shut up, or pointing out that you've still got a long way to go before you're as successful as Steve Jobs, or as popular as the Pope.

Cheerleaders are essential when you're applying for new jobs; they'll keep your spirits up and give you a strong shot of confidence. They're also vital during break-ups and at the beginning of new relationships, because they're your personal P.R. powerhouse. If you believe you're half as amazing as they think you are, you can take over the world before lunch.

If they're your Cheerleader, you're their Inspiration.

The Wise Owl (Proudlock)

These feathered friends don't always tell you what you want to hear, but they're very good at showing you what you need to know. It can be a bit of a thankless job for them, so make sure you show your appreciation, even if they're telling you off.

The Wise Owl is one of those people who has the gift of insight. They are very good at standing back from situations and getting a serious, objective perspective. They have a strong sense of justice and they always know who's in the right and who is in the wrong. However, they're born diplomats and they'll appeal to your better nature before they try to shame you. If you were to write something in a thought bubble coming out of the Wise Owl's mind, it would be, *I'm not angry, I'm just very disappointed.* Wise Owls are the ones who make us better people, and they're brave enough to call you out and force you to do the right thing, even if they know that you might be quite grumpy about it.

Being cross with the Wise Owl is a waste of time, because they're always right, which is maddening, but reassuring. However, a Wise Owl isn't simply a modern-day Jiminy Cricket with a WhatsApp account. They're also invaluable when you're making any serious decision. If you're thinking about changing flatmates, breaking up with someone or dealing with a problem at work, the Wise Owl will guide you through the process. They don't want to make your life easier, but they do want to help you to make it better.

Proudlock makes a great Wise Owl when I have love trouble, because he's the friend who will tell it like it is. He's the only friend who won't pretend the boy I like isn't texting anymore because he accidentally dropped his phone off the side of a boat.

A genuine Wise Owl is worth their weight in Gucci. Beware, though – there are plenty of fake Owls who are not good friends. They just love being a bit bossy and using their claws to rip you apart. A true Owl will refrain from giving you advice unless you have specifically asked for it. When you find your wise friend, treasure them, because genuine wisdom is in shorter supply than available power sockets in your local Pret.

If they're your Wise Owl, you're their Naughty One.

The Gossip Girl – or Boy (Alex)

Be completely honest with me. You love a good gossip, don't you? We pretend that it's a bit gross and grubby, and we're all too high minded for it, but gossip makes the world go around. Gossip puts the bubbles in life's champagne bottle. It's petrol! When you have a friend who is gifted at gossiping, be grateful for them. Their conversation usually sparkles. They're more gripping than any box set.

In its purest form, gossip isn't usually mean, and there's a big difference between true gossip, and going behind someone's back. Your gossiper isn't malicious, and they're not spreading information because they're seeking to hurt anyone. They're just fascinated by the way humans work, and they want to share that fascination with a keen audience.

My friend Alex Mytton is a classic gossip, because he simply can't keep anything to himself. Gossip is currency, and it helps you to feel connected with all of your other friends. In a way, it's no different from being a newspaper columnist. When I wrote my *Style* column, I gave opinions based on what I care about, but a lot of that comes from gossip about my life, and other people's. When people write pieces about what Theresa May has just done, and what they think she's going to do next, that's gossip, albeit a kind that comes from a very informed place. If you know and love a Gossip Girl or Boy, there's a strong chance that they're a journalist. Again, be careful about the Gossips you choose to be close to, because some are cruel, and they do want to use their powers for evil. If someone is very insecure about themselves, they can gossip for all the wrong reasons, using other people's information to make themselves feel bigger and better. Avoid these people as much as possible.

Also, be aware that Gossips will want some information about you in return. Be very careful about what you tell them. If you don't share anything, they will soon stop gossiping with you – just stay alert and be very deliberate. For example, if you're having a sexy, scandalous fling with a deposed Italian count, spill! If you've got a persistent case of thrush that is mystifying your G.P., you might want to keep that information to yourself. If you keep squirming in the seat, simply tell the Gossip Girl or Boy that you're excited about what they're going to tell next!

If they're your Gossip Girl, you're their Flirt.

The Naughty One (Jess)

I love my Naughty friends with all my heart, although, as the name suggests, they are always getting me into trouble. Quite a lot of us make a Naughty chum before we start school. If you had an imaginary friend who was forced to take the blame for spills, spoiled dinners and broken vases, your craving for a Naughty pal was so great that you had to invent one.

This is why we need the Naughty Ones. We're all dealing with dozens of different impulses all day long, and there's a constant fight between what we think we should do and what we really want to do. Now, we all know that we can't just do what we want all the time. If I did that, I'd be barefoot at a festival right now, covered in glitter and paying for a round of vodka for thirty people, while demanding that everyone at the bar start a conga line. I'm enough of a grown-up to know that desks need sitting at, vegetables need eating and even bedtimes need observing occasionally. However, you need your Naughty friends to remind you to be a child occasionally, and to tell you that a dose of fun is an important part of a life well lived.

My naughtiest friends are probably Jess and Ollie. I don't think any of us are especially naughty when we're on our own, but when we're together in any combination, it turns into one of those mad chemical experiments where relatively stable elements fizz, whoosh and set the school lab on fire. Naughty friends are the ones who don't believe in bedtimes. Tell a Naughty friend that you're going home at eleven, and they'll laugh like you're Jack Whitehall and they're in the audience for *Live at the Apollo*. Naughty friends have a sixth sense for those slightly dodgy drinking dens, and bars that turn out to be the sitting rooms of strangers. Also, they dance as though they're in the throes of demonic possession. They don't care about looking cool, sexy or impressive, they just want to have fun. With you. When you wake up in the morning feeling as though someone is cutting your hair with a chainsaw, your mouth tastes like the bottom of a bin and you're pretty sure you've been smooching someone, but you have no idea what they're initials are, the Naughty friend has struck.

The best Naughty friends are the ones who are relatively sensible and good when you're not around. If your friend is constantly misbehaving, it might be time to start keeping an eye on them. Constant boozing and regular late nights just aren't good for the body, soul or psyche, and unless your friend is actually Keith Richards, they might be using their naughtiness to mask some bigger problem. Use your intuition – if you think that the partying has gone from fun to excessive, it might be time for you to become their Wise Owl, or even their Cheerleader, and show them that they can be fun and lovely without racking up a four-figure bar bill. Similarly, if everyone thinks of you as the Naughty One, it might be time for a night in.

If they're your Naughty One, you're their Wise Owl.

The Inspiration (Mark-Francis)

Some of your friends should stretch and challenge you. We all need people who push us, who can show us how to become the very best versions of ourselves. Find a friend who is truly gifted at Instagram, and they can show you the true secrets of good living!

Mark-Francis is an Inspiration for me in many ways. He inspires me with his style. I think he's the only person who comes close to being almost as stylish as Granny Denise. He's perfectly turned out, and he makes me want to reach for the cashmere and get out the heated rollers instead of scraping my hair back and hiding under a cap. He also inspires me to really *look around* and find beauty in everything I see. London is so overwhelming that it's easy to miss so much of it. Mark has shown me that you don't have to go to a gallery to see a work of art. We'll be in a taxi and he'll tell me about the Roman history of the London Wall, or point out a statue or sculpture that dates back to medieval times. I'm obsessed with politics and current affairs, but Mark inspires me to learn about the past as well as the present, and shows me that it's much more exciting to live in London if you know about the art and culture that connects the place with its people.

> 6 A night out with my best friends is better for me than spending a week in the gym. 9

I'm not sure I'll ever match his 24/7 approach to elegance, but I can't help but admire the fact that he's never watching television in his jogging bottoms. I like to look nice, but he lives like an artist and puts aesthetics before anything or anyone else. While I don't think I could ever live exactly as he does, he certainly makes me want to put more of an effort into everything, whether it's choosing something beautiful to put on my walls or ensuring that I always have beautifully laundered socks.

Inspiring friends aren't necessarily the people who make us feel as though we should be just like they are. They are usually incredibly secure, and they don't need anyone to copy them in order to validate their life choices. One of the most inspiring things about them is their honesty. They don't pretend that their considerable success is an accident. They show us that great things can be achieved when you work hard, but also that the hard work is essential. To be honest, I'm inspired by everyone on *Made in Chelsea*, and their work on the programme often represents a small part of their drive, ambition and determination. Everyone has a passion project that they work at conscientiously, and when people are really striving to make something happen, it usually takes off.

Inspirational friends aren't there to completely alter the way we live, but they do make us evaluate our own ambitions and consider our priorities. They show us what's possible when we focus, and make us realize what we might need to sacrifice in order to pursue our dreams. Ultimately, your Inspiration should make you feel the opposite emotions to a toxic social-media binge. Time spent with an Inspiration should be nourishing and exciting, not draining and confusing. Think of an Inspiration as the lobster cocktail on the buffet table of friendship. A little of their company makes everything seem much more luxurious, but too much will seem overwhelming and you might have to go for a lie down.

If they're your Inspiration, you're their Cheerleader.

The Grown-Up (Stanley Johnson)
I would say that I have always been drawn to the Grown-Ups. This

is partly due to my personality. There's something deeply reassuring about being around proper adults who don't mess about. A Grown-Up can be enormously silly, but they don't waste their time and energy on pursuing nonsense. They love dirty jokes and daft puns, but they're not going to have petty arguments with dinner, stop speaking to people in order to punish them, or devote any time to the trivial things that make life less than pleasant.

My friend Stanley is the ultimate Grown-Up. When you're in your seventies, you've seen pretty much everything, and you're great at knowing what is actually important and what's simply too silly to bother with. I think this is Stanley in a nutshell. He's a great friend, because he won't be cross with me for being slightly late for lunch, because he knows that's a waste of his time. However, he will make sure I know that being very late, very often is a sign of great immaturity, and he doesn't have enough time left on earth to sit on his own in restaurants, when he has better things to do.

Some Grown-Ups have been married and divorced more than once, and they are great at giving you a dose of tough love when you're waiting for a boy to arrange a third date. Essentially, they're social historians who know what to say when your anxiety is going into overdrive. They have decades over you, and tons of personal experience, and they aren't going to let you waste your time worrying, as they once did. Grown-Ups have their priorities in order. That's not to say they're serious. Most Grown-Ups have arrived at a point in their life when they're ready for fun. That's where you come in. They're the bosses of their lives, and sometimes bosses of entire companies, too. They know how to be responsible, and now they're looking for ways to shake off that responsibility and go dancing.

A Grown-Up isn't to be confused with a Wise Owl. There are many similarities, but your relationship with a Grown-Up will probably be slightly more symbiotic. They can tell you whether you need to worry about pensions, and how to get them, but they might need you to help them navigate their Spotify playlist. Grown-Ups usually have a few years on you, but sometimes they're simply someone with an exceptionally mature attitude. A true Grown-Up is never bossy. If a Grown-Up friend is determined to tell you what to do, they're not really a friend at all, they're just extremely irritating.

If they're your Grown-Up, you're their Naughty One.

The Flirt (Sam Thompson)

The final category is possibly the hardest one to get right, but when you crack it, you've got the best sort of friend a girl could have. The flirty friend offers you a very different sort of ego boost from the Cheerleader, but it's still essential. Let me be very clear: you don't want a relationship with the Flirt, and they cannot want one with you, either. If one of you is secretly carrying a torch for the other, it will turn into a dreadful bonfire of doom, leaving you with the friendship equivalent of tragic dead hedgehogs. No one wants that. There can be no power play in a flirty friendship. It's not about sexy intentions, but it's all connected with the way you communicate.

Sam has always been a flirty friend of mine, and I think this might be connected with the fact that we were both quite young when we became mates. As teenagers, we'd flirt with everyone. I was a couple of years away from evolving to the point of having best friends who were boys, and I think I flirted with everyone I met, just in case something exciting happened. Sam was the same. When we chat, we have a real spark, but that really begins and ends with our conversation. I don't think it would work in any other setting.

Sam and I have always been incredibly close, and once, when he'd been sleeping in my bed (in an entirely innocent way), he walked down the hallway and my housemates discovered that he had an entire piece of pizza stuck to his bum. I used to eat a lot of pizza in bed, and I suppose it was inevitable that the odd slice would go astray. Still, if you want to make Sam go bright red, tell him he stinks of pepperoni and have a good look at his bum.

Flirty friends are like tennis partners. When you talk to each other, you're trying to keep a ball in the air, and you're trying to serve it to them in the most stylish way possible. Also, with a Flirt, you don't feel as though you're making too much of an effort to keep things light and fun. It all happens naturally. The perfect Flirt is someone who will take you out for a glass of champagne after a difficult day. They won't encourage you to moan or complain, and you'll dress up as though you're going on a date, but you won't have any nerves or scary expectations. You'll both go home uplifted and feeling loved, and you know they'll text you the next day.

The only problem with flirty friends is that they can be very difficult to maintain. If one of you is in a relationship and the other one is single, the new partner might understandably feel threatened by the flirty friend – and whoever is single will feel bad that their old buddy is now spending all their time with someone who flirts with them seriously. If you're both single and at least one of you would like to be in a relationship, at some point a drunken snog is inevitable. Remember – Richard Curtis is not directing your life! Hooking up with your friends is not part of a charming film script that ends with you covered in confetti, wearing Emma Hope slippers. It usually ends in you losing a friend. One way to keep the balance is to make sure you and your flirty friend have secondary functions in each other's lives – try to give each other genuinely useful advice and helpful perspective. To put it bluntly, one of you needs to be the Grown-Up.

If they're your Flirt, you're their Grown-Up.

When to break up with a friend

Most of us know when and how to end a romantic relationship: when kissing them starts to remind you of getting chewing gum out of your back teeth, when their name on your caller ID makes your heart sink, or when you can see them walking up your street and you hide behind the sofa and turn all of the lights off. But ending a friendship is much harder. This is partly because our expectations for friendship are different. It's not an all-consuming relationship, and so it's pretty savage to have to say, 'Sorry, but

I don't want to drink wine on Tuesdays with you any more. We assume that friendships can only be ended if one party has done something completely awful.

The trouble is that, when it comes to friends and where we find them, we're spoiled for choice. As well as school friends and neighbours, we have work friends, which is fine if we're employed by the same company for ten years, and much trickier to manage if we have projects and side hustles, and some kind of new job every six months. We travel and date more than any other generation, and we're constantly meeting new people, which is enormously exciting, but it demands a lot of our time. It's easy to grow apart from people. Sometimes, we get to a point where we realize it's better to have a few friends we have plenty in common with than a cast of thousands who we only see for half an hour once a year, before backing out the door, yelling, 'Next time, we must have a proper catch up!'

Firstly, it's natural to fall out with your friends, just as it's OK to fall out of love with someone. Most of the time, you'll make it up, but occasionally you'll realize that you and your former friend have completely different values, desires and agendas. If you feel as though you're constantly making compromises for the sake of a friendship, it might be time to accept that you don't have enough in common to keep the relationship afloat. If your housemate constantly wants you to stay in and keep her company on a Friday night, but she's never prepared to join you on the dance floor, it might be time to call time. If you go on a girls' holiday to Portugal every year, even though the girls keep promising that next year will be the ski trip you long for, that friendship isn't serving you.

On *Made in Chelsea*, most of the big friendship fall-outs are a result of two things: romance gone wrong, and people stabbing each other in the back and getting found out. There is usually quite a lot of crossover between the two, and the fall-outs happen on a grand scale, as everyone takes sides. Occasionally, I think the drama is used as an excuse. If you've decided someone isn't for you, and you don't know how to tell them that you've grown apart, it's easier to wait until something serious has happened and claim that's why you're no longer speaking to someone – even though that's not necessarily the truth. For example, it was much easier for me to be furious with Sam Prince for having sex in my bed than to simply say I was finding him a bit boring as a romantic prospect. (We're still good pals, though . . .)

Anyway, I can stay friends with anyone as long as they are capable of two very important things: kindness and making me laugh. I think humour is a vital part of any relationship, but it's enormously subjective, too. Remember this. Never dump a friend by telling them they have shit chat. Simply say, 'I just don't think we are comically compatible.' Here are some of the signs to watch out for, if you're starting to think a friendship might be over:

- You find it really hard to be pleased for them when something good happens – for example, they announce their engagement, and you start to imagine 'accidentally' spilling red wine on their wedding dress.
- If they post something new on social media, you won't 'like' it before checking that they liked your last picture.

- Spending time with them gives you backache, because it makes your shoulders so tense.
- If they can't come for dinner because they're broke, or they've lost their wallet, you claim you can't pay for them because you've given all of your money to an African prince who emailed you with an exciting investment opportunity.
- You only ever invite them out if you know they're on holiday in Mauritius and will be a fourteen-hour plane journey away from you.
- Even though you have the same friends and enemies in common, you start thinking about befriending the people you know they don't like.

The point of this checklist is to spot the signs of a friendship gone bad, and to make sure you act on them before the relationship turns totally toxic. This isn't about you hating your old friend, or the idea that you're right and they're wrong. It's important to recognize that you've grown apart, and it was a no-fault accident. It's as if the sun got into your eyes while you were driving, and you've pranged your car on the pavement. There is no point being angry with yourself, and no point getting cross with the car behind you, either.

Be brave. It's easy to simply stop calling your friend, and to hide away, hoping they've got the message. This is pretty cowardly, though. Think about how horrible it is when you get ghosted, and the person you've been seeing for weeks suddenly stops replying. It's not fair to do that to a friend or a lover. You need to make a date and talk about what's going on.

Approach the situation with an open mind. When one of my friends started to get on my nerves a bit, I didn't stop to wonder whether something serious was going on. I just decided she was irritating me, and I wanted out. However, when we talked, she told me that she'd been having a really stressful time at work, and that had been making her a bit needy and boring. I'd been so focused on my own grumpy feelings, I hadn't thought about hers. Our friendship just needed a bit of recalibration. The worst thing you can do in any relationship is to assume that you know what's going on, without asking about it. Sometimes, you can save things just by speaking out.

However, if you have a chat and it's clear that you're simply headed in different directions, don't be afraid to say so. The whole point of the exercise is to avoid unnecessary drama – our lives have enough of the unavoidable stuff as it is, we really don't need any extra.

A few years ago, you could have kept in touch with a few close school friends and been happy to let everyone else go. You could wish them well, but you didn't need to remain close to them. However, now that most of us are constantly online, it's impossible to let these friendships simply fade away. Every time someone you were at school with goes on holiday, you're alerted to it. If you were in someone's geography class in 2007, you'll have a chance to look through their wedding pictures. It's bizarre, and it means that most of us feel overwhelmed by our friends.

I'm really fortunate because I'm still incredibly close to Amy, who was my very best chum at school and still is. In some ways,

Amy is my opposite. At school, I was quite a good girl and I followed the rules most of the time, but Amy was the one who sneaked out and inspired me to be naughty. She's very practical, and great to have around in a crisis, even if her solutions can be a bit short term . . .

My favourite Amy story took place after Christmas, when we were about fifteen. My mum had moved into a penthouse apartment. I think we'd had our Christmas tree delivered, but we had no way of getting it out of the flat. Amy decided that the only thing to do was to throw it out of the window, off the balcony. I'll never forget watching her huffing and puffing – at one point, it looked like she was having a sexy slow dance with the tree. She managed to get it over the ledge, but then it bounced, and got stuck on someone's roof for *months*. Christmas comes but once a year, but our unlucky neighbour was stuck with a fun, festive reminder until summer. To be honest, that's a great analogy for friendships that go on for too long. Amy is a forever friend, but some people stick around for the sake of tradition – like a Christmas tree that's stuck on the roof, well into the new year.

I think the biggest friendship issue that most of us face in our twenties comes from keeping up with old school friends. When you're fourteen, you can find common ground with pretty much everyone in your year. You all have exactly the same interests and lifestyles. You want to finish your homework with minimal stress, plan something fun for the summer holidays and work out whether your French teacher really is having a thrilling secret fling with the head of Games. Until you're eighteen, these people are your world. Then, you leave, and some of you go off to university – and the next time you see each other, half of you have got engaged, or retrained as an accountant, or run off to Barcelona. You don't appreciate how little you know someone until you realize that they have voluntarily decided to devote their adult life to maths.

Family and V.I.P.s

Grandad Bertie: the big softie

I'm really fortunate to have so many amazing men in my life, but one of the most brilliant and best is my mum's dad, Grandad Bertie. He's a human encyclopaedia who knows everything about everything. He's constantly inspiring me with his humour, enthusiasm, and passion for life – he's *always* checking out birds! No, not what you're thinking; he's a keen ornithologist! He keeps a pair of binoculars in his car (also known as the Toffmobile!) and, as well as being able to spot a birds' nest from a mile away, he knows when the bird will be coming back – in the same way he seems to know when I'm coming back to Devon, before I do! It's like a spooky sixth sense.

He's always been my hero, and I think he's one of the bravest people in the world. Last summer, he fought off robbers when he was in Spain with Granny! Grandad was reading the paper when he noticed a lady had left her handbag behind. Being a Good Samaritan, he ran after her, but she pushed him in a doorway, they scuffled and she grabbed his watch! She jumped in a car with two young men in it, so Grandad punched the driver at the wheel, who yelled, 'Give the crazy man his watch back!' She did! He'd had his watch forty years and wasn't going to lose it without a fight, even if it was three against one!

Still, he's really a big softie. There's no one else who would get up at midnight and drive around for an hour in order to find me a Burger King Whopper. He also makes the best poached eggs on the planet, which must be eaten on white bread. I'd rather eat Bertie's poached eggs than go to Scott's for supper. He is also, mysteriously, a whizz at ASOS returns. Nanny is constantly ordering from ASOS and then deciding the clothes are too young for her, which is *obviously nonsense* – but, as soon as she knows something is going back, Bertie is filling in the forms with a Biro and folding everything up to go back in the bag. He's made some of his best friends in the Post Office, he spends so much time there!

Most of all, he's kind. He really wants everyone to do well, and he doesn't envy anyone. He cares about politics and wants to make sure that everyone's voice is heard. He will never mince his words and he prides himself on saying exactly what's on his mind, but he always does it with humour and love. The only thing that frustrates him is time wasters. I think this is because he has such energy and enthusiasm, he can't bear to waste a single second and doesn't understand anyone who can!

Granny Denise: my style icon

Other than my mum, the woman who has been the greatest influence on my life is probably Granny Denise. While most of my BFFs are boys, these ladies have played the biggest role when it comes to shaping me and helping me to become the woman I am today. If you've ever watched *Made in Chelsea*, you'd probably recognize Granny straight away. She's even joined me on *Celebs Go Dating*. After all, I could never get serious about anyone if Denise didn't approve!

My granny has been with my grandad since before I was born, but she's not biologically related to me. Mum was just fifteen years old when her mum passed away, and Grandad married Denise a few years later. Anyone who has seen me and my granny together would probably be shocked to discover that she doesn't actually share any genes with my mum and me. Granny and I are incredibly similar, although I'm definitely not nearly as glamorous as she is. She's the person I want to be when I grow up, and she's a fashion expert. She knows her Prada from her Peter Pilotto.

Granny and Grandad Bertie are the embodiment of my absolute relationship goal. Seeing them together makes me realize there is absolutely no point in settling. My grandad is besotted with Denise, and I think that, if anything, he adores her slightly more now than he did on the day they met. He's an absolute legend. Even though he's just turned eighty, I don't think he'll ever slow down. They both get a lot of love on Instagram, and they're constantly starring in my Stories.

Granny is my style icon. I might long to dress like Coco Chanel, or wish I could put an outfit together as elegantly as Audrey Hepburn, but Granny makes the most legendary chic women look as though they had five minutes to get dressed in a church jumble sale, in the middle of a power cut. She is the colour queen and, in her world, nothing is simply pink or blue. She's more likely to say, 'Georgia, did you see? They had the most divine eau de Nil blouse on the third floor of Harrods!' She has a real passion for cerise, too – a very particular, grown-up shade of hot pink that is *not* to be confused with mauve or magenta. That said, there was one year when she dressed entirely in black and looked brilliant in it. While I love a LBD, if I wear too many dark colours, people see me and start humming *The Addams Family* theme tune, but Granny looked much more glamorous than goth. I'm glad she's back in pastels now, though, because I love our baby pinks and blues. This is why I wear so many pretty candy colours: I'm channelling Denise.

Mum and Granny are incredibly close, and usually see eye to eye, especially on matters of style, but very occasionally there's a bit of a conflict. Well, once. And it was bra based. I was eleven and *longing* for a bra. Obviously, I had *nothing* to put in one. Even now, there are more Kettle Chips in a paleo dieter's cupboard than there are actual boobs in my bra, if I'm honest. I am the chicken-fillet queen! Still, even though any sensible person would have known that I had several vest-wearing years still ahead of me, bras seemed glamorous and grown-up, and I really wanted one. When I mentioned it to Mum, I think she laughed me out of the room. I was so young that she probably thought she'd be buying bras for my Barbies before she had to think about an awkward trip to M & S to see the lady with the tape measure.

However, I had an ace up my sleeve – or, rather, my lacy strap. Previous experience had taught me that, if Mum told me I was too young to have what I wanted, Granny would usually oblige. So, I waited until we were visiting my grandparents in Spain, whispered the magic words and suddenly Granny and I were on our way to the poshest lingerie shop in the local *galleria*.

Usually, a girl's first bra looks as though it's been made out of her Games kit. It's sensible, practical, comes in one of fifty shades of beige and is slightly less sexy than a hiking cagoule. However, most girls don't get Denise's expertise when they're on their bra-buying expedition. I came home with a tiny, embroidered scrap of lace, and my very first pair of chicken fillets. My mum was horrified. 'She's far too young! What have you done?' she whimpered.

Denise was unrepentant: 'Well, she'll thank me in the future.'

I looked down at my non-existent boobs, assuming that she was about to explain that she'd stopped me from going down the road of a saggy cleavage. Nothing so practical.

'She'll always know it's of the utmost importance to have beautiful, high-quality lingerie.'

I'm not sure that Mum was convinced.

You'd think that Granny's efforts would have ensured that

I'm the kind of girl who always wears gorgeous, matching bra and knicker sets, for the benefit of the paramedics who might see them if I get run over, if no one else. However, while I love the look of sexy underwear, I've made my peace with the fact that, when it comes to pants, I'm basically Bridget Jones. When you're running around Chelsea all day long, sexy underwear is just scratchy underwear. You can't dance in a thong, although it can help you reach the high notes when you're singing along at karaoke. I'm never happier than when I'm in really big knickers. In fact, I think the ultimate pair would be knickers that come all the way over your nipples, so you don't need to bother with a bra – you can just pull them all the way up to your armpits and head out the door!

Anyway, Granny's attitude to beauty is decidedly old school, and she believes you have to suffer if you want to look beautiful. I'm with her, up to a point. I have nothing but respect for Granny, Mum and their hairdresser. They've been seeing the same lady in Battersea for years, and they spend whole days getting their highlights done. (Granny *hated* my hairbrush-free years. If I close my eyes, I can still see her holding a comb, with a look of long-suffering patience plastered to her face, as she attempts to do battle with my enormous knots.) I even agree with her about taking all your

> **When Mum tells me she's proud of me, it means more than any other achievement, job or compliment.**

make-up off before you go to bed. OK, I might not actually always *do* it, but I definitely think she's on to something.

However, I'm only ever prepared to suffer for about an hour at a time. Granny can wear heels all day and look amazing. I can manage a few minutes before the pain hits, and I'm back in my stinky, knackered and gloriously comfy Air Force Ones. The face Granny makes when she sees me in these trainers is *amazing*. Imagine you've just run yourself a hot bath after a rubbish day, and you'd been dreaming of luxurious, scented bubbles for hours – but, as soon as you step into the water, you realize the boiler has broken, and someone has replaced your gorgeous Jo Malone Pomegranate Noir with Fairy Liquid. *That's* Granny's trainer face.

Still, there's so much more to Granny than her style-icon status. She and Mum have worked so hard to show me how to be a lady, and it's not just about getting dressed up. The point is that I *can* wear my trainers, and still feel just as classy as I would in a pair of court shoes. It's all about having the right attitude, which comes down to working very hard, being very kind and striving to see the funny side of everything.

Mum and Dad: how can I ever thank them enough?

While Granny and Grandad have always spoiled me a bit, my mum and dad have both taught me that it's incredibly important not to take anything for granted. Neither of my parents grew up with a lot of wealth and privilege, and they worked incredibly hard to give me as many advantages as they could – but they always thought it was more important to spend money on my education than on handbags and holidays. I meet an amazing mix of people from a variety of backgrounds, but it always shocks me to realize that some people have never really struggled, and they've always been given everything they want. I'm so, so privileged. I get to live in a lovely little flat by myself, in my favourite part of London, and I could put on three layers of clothes every single day and never run out of things to wear, but I feel as though I appreciate it all the more because it's not the world I grew up in. The best lesson my mum taught me was to be content, and that being ambitious was important, but it was just as important to value everything I had, instead of demanding more.

Mum also showed me that the best reason to be ambitious is that it makes you more independent. Even though her dad ran a very successful business, she wanted to be successful in her own right, so she started a property-development company. She split up with my dad when I was a baby because she knew that the relationship wasn't working, and that they would be better parents to me by being apart. The greatest thing she's done for me is to show me that it's better to want other people than to need them. I think this is where all of my drive comes from. Mum has shown me that, when you take charge of your own life and set goals for yourself, you can do absolutely everything, and you don't need to depend on anyone else for your success. She's taught me how to love my own company. In fact, I think I'm so sociable because I choose to spend time with people I like, because I want to see them. I don't need anyone else to validate me.

When Mum tells me she's proud of me, it means more than any other achievement, job or compliment. When I went into the jungle, even though I knew that the whole country could be watching, her opinion mattered more than anyone else's. That moment when she surprised me in the jungle will always be one of the very best moments of my life. I'd been having such a brilliant time, and everything was so new and strange that I didn't realize how much I'd been missing her. I still feel weepy when I think about what it was like to hug her after so long.

Mum and Dad both care so much about keeping me grounded. I know they're incredibly excited about my career and my achievements, but they're also very concerned about making sure that I don't tie my self-worth completely to my work. At the moment, I think they're really pleased because I'm doing what I love, I'm working really hard and I'm excited about it. But they'd be just as pleased and excited for me if I was still cleaning loos in an office, if that was my true passion. (Seriously, it is a necessary job. I think everybody should work as a loo cleaner at some point in their lives. I do recommend a sturdy pair of gloves, though.)

From the outside, my family might seem complicated and confusing, but I constantly feel lucky to have all of these brilliant people in my life. Because I don't have any brothers or sisters, I revel in the fact that I have a brilliant stepdad, a host of extra aunties and cousins, and people who show me, every day, that family goes beyond biology. It's just about loving each other and making each other laugh.

Toff's top tips for meeting the parents, grandparents and other V.I.P.s

If you want to be my lover, or my friend, you have to be able to get on with my family. These are the most important people in my life, and bonding with them is a non-negotiable issue. To be honest, the most important thing for me is that you try. But if you really want to win me over, here's a cheat sheet for winning them over, too. I'm pretty sure that most of these tips will work in any meet-the-family situation, so it doesn't matter who you're meeting, most of these are worth a try.

Make an effort
In my family, everyone likes to get dressed up for special occasions, even if the occasion is simply, 'It's Tuesday!' Looking good will go a long way when it comes to making a great impression, especially if you're meeting my grandparents. However, this isn't necessarily the time to be trendy. You might have spent a fortune on a pair of pre-ripped, distressed jeans, but my grandfather will simply look you up and down and ask you whether you have just been dragged through a hedge backwards, or if the dragging went in multiple directions. Keep it simple and clean. Polish your shoes,

check for loose threads and, if you wear tights, make sure they're ladder free. If you're meeting anyone's family, it's always worth making sure your outfit is modest and fully windproof: you want to make sure there's zero risk of anyone seeing your underwear on your first meeting, whatever the weather.

Be respectful

To me, my granny is basically a celebrity. Whenever I speak to my mum, she's always excited to tell me about what Granny's been up to and what she's wearing, and she imparts the information with the same levels of seriousness as a news reporter talking about Meghan Markle's upcoming royal tour. So, when you meet my family, or anyone's family, you need to treat the occasion as though you were going to have dinner with the Queen at Elton John's house. You want to make a brilliant impression, but you have to remember that this is all about them. Ask them about themselves, don't talk over them, and always ask before taking any pictures.

Find some fabulous flowers

It doesn't matter how young at heart the grown-ups in a family might seem – they're all old-fashioned enough to love receiving flowers when you're visiting them and, more to the point, they'll expect them. Come without flowers and you might as well turn up at the door with some dog poo that has been rolled up in a newspaper and set alight. Even if the recipient has crippling hay fever, or a leaf allergy, they'd rather see you brandishing a bunch of petrol-station carnations than watch you turn up empty-handed.

In my family, everyone loves bright colours, so, if you want a gold star, find flowers that are yellow, orange, pink and purple. Possibly, all in the same bouquet. The one exception is those weird dyed flowers with rainbow-striped petals. Everyone finds them quite unsettling. (Irrationally, I'm always slightly worried that they have been genetically modified and might have eyes and teeth, too.)

Tell a joke

If you're stuck for something to say, the very best thing you can do is make people laugh. Even if the joke is truly terrible, it will act as a bit of an icebreaker and it shows that you're prepared to make an effort to be entertaining. Everyone loves a dad joke, especially my grandad, who has been a dad for decades. In fact, you can make a joke *of* dad jokes: Why is it inappropriate to make a dad joke if you're not a dad? It's a *faux pa*!

Mind your manners

Lots of people think that etiquette is to do with knowing when to use a luncheon knife and only wearing brown shoes in the country, or never wearing gloves after three p.m. on a rainy day. This is part of it (apart from the gloves thing – I made that up), but the whole point of good manners is to put people at their ease and make them feel comfortable. Admittedly, if you're meeting the entire Toff clan, you might be the one who needs to be put at ease, but that doesn't mean that you can't try to raise your politeness game.

If you've had a meal at someone's house, get up and help as

> ❝ Grandad Bertie is really a big softie. There's no-one else who would get up at midnight and drive around for an hour in order to find me a Burger King Whopper. ❞

soon as someone starts clearing the table. Don't say, 'May I help?' because they'll feel obliged to tell you to sit down, and that doesn't leave an impression on anything but the chair supporting your lazy bum. If you're meeting people in a pub, buy a round of drinks. My grandad is a very generous man, but he's not impressed by anyone who doesn't stand their round. Also, if you're stuck for conversation, ask people about the book they're reading, the last film they watched or whether they're in the middle of any box sets. The only thing most people love more than their own opinions is meeting people who are interested in hearing them.

Give good compliments

As you might have guessed, if you want to find the way to my granny's heart, simply tell her how much you love her outfit. Be specific and ask lots of questions. She won't just say thank you, she will give you the specific coordinates of where the skirt was hanging in Harvey Nichols, or how she saw it in *Vogue* and had to keep calling Selfridges until they told her it had come in. This doesn't just work for fashion. If you're meeting the family and they've cooked, they'll be desperate to tell you where they found

45

the recipe, or how they picked their curtains, or where they were standing in that lovely photo that's hanging in the hall.

Keep smiling

Positivity is the very best thing that you can bring to any family situation, especially if you're meeting mine. The Toffs are born smilers, and if you turn up with a cheerful grin, they will accept you as one of their own. It's pretty much impossible to see a person smiling and not smile back, so if you're scared and the situation seems super serious, fake it, and keep the corners of your mouth upturned until everyone is beaming and you don't have to pretend anymore!

Beyond the family

While my family are definitely the ones who are responsible for making me into the woman I am, there are so many incredible people who have inspired me every day, over the last few years. These are the ones who make me feel lucky, every single day. I love my life and my job, and the reason that I feel so fortunate is that the work I do has led me to these amazing, inspiring people. Also, my career is something that I have to make up as I go along. I don't get appraisals, I don't really have a line manager and there's no annual Christmas party where there's a risk that I'll get drunk and photocopy my bum. (This is the very first thing I'd do if I was in the same room as alcohol and a photocopier. In fact, I can imagine myself having too many Jägerbombs and trying to *fax* my bum, eighties style.) Anyway, because I don't have anyone telling me what to do, I'm always looking for role models and good examples – even if those good examples can sometimes be very naughty! These people have all helped me along the path to adulthood, and I owe them all enormous hugs and lots of big drinks.

Emily and Lottie

These women are two of my very best friends, and I have more fun with them than almost anyone else. A night out with Emily and Lottie is better for me than spending a week in the gym. They make me ache so much from laughing that sometimes I think I need a tube of Deep Heat afterwards. However, they're also kind, wise and full of great advice. Like me, Lottie chose to pursue her career instead of finishing a degree, and Lottie is the one who reminds me that I made the right choice. Even more importantly, she shows me that it *is* a choice, and that I'm the one who has control over everything I do.

Emily and Lottie are just as ambitious as I am, and they constantly show me that it's an extremely exciting time to be a confident woman who is motivated to build a bright future. They both work so hard, which means that, when they have free time, they don't waste a single second when it comes to enjoying it. Also, they both give brilliant advice and they're super straight-talking. Emily will always tell me what I need to hear, even if it isn't what I want to hear. Lottie won't let me play it safe; she says that, when it comes to work, you have to do things that scare you, and she's usually

47

right. Most importantly, they both make me focus on looking forward and thinking about all of the exciting stuff on the horizon. When I make a mistake, they're the ones who help me to put it into perspective and make me realize that what's happened in the past doesn't have to define the future.

Ollie

Darling Ollie is a member of my family, to all intents and purposes. His house in Fulham is where I go when I need to rest, relax and chill out, even though a quiet night with Netflix often ends in copious amounts of gin, and snogging on the kitchen table. Ollie inspires me with his kindness. He shows me how important it is to be generous – not just with money and gifts, but with time. No matter how busy Ollie is, he always makes time for his friends and puts them first. He also shows me how important it is to celebrate the people you love. Ollie knows that it's just as important to be a cheerleader and get excited about your friends' achievements as it is to be there for them when times are tough.

My Made in Chelsea *family*

Being on a reality show has been a strange, wonderful, hilarious and emotional part of my education, and when you find yourself in so many odd and lovely situations with people, you have to think of them as your family. The cast members all inspire me to work as hard as I can, and to embrace every single opportunity that comes my way. Also, being on the show has helped me to own my emotions. I think we all wear our hearts on our sleeves, and I know that bottling things up never helps anyone. It's OK to have the odd meltdown, and you usually feel much better for it.

The This Morning crew

Holly, Phil and the *This Morning* team might not have been in my life for that long, but, my goodness, they have already taught me so much! I watch Holly like a hawk. I think she has such an impressive, exciting career, and what she doesn't know about presenting and camerawork simply isn't worth knowing. Every single person on the set has made me want to raise my professional game. It doesn't matter if it's so early in the morning that it feels like the middle of the night, or if your shoes hurt, or if you're having a bad hair day. Now I know that I have to keep smiling and trying my hardest, because I've got the chance to do the most exciting job in the world. Holly and Phil are such skilled interviewers, too, and they have taught me how to ask questions naturally and use research as a prompt. It's important to know what you're talking about, but it's always better to react and listen to your gut than to stick rigidly to a script.

My campmates

You simply can't go to the other side of the world with a group of people that you've never met and not be inspired by them. Even on *Made in Chelsea*, where I have the chance to work with a wide variety of people, everyone has a fairly similar background to mine. In the jungle, I had the chance to learn from people who came from completely different places, experiences and generations. Of course, Stanley was the one I bonded with straight away, but I loved the fact that I could have conversations with people like Amir and Iain, who I'd never have met anywhere else, and their perspectives were completely different from mine. Everyone showed me how important it was to persevere, and that it was possible to seem completely confident one day and extremely vulnerable the next. I loved how Rebekah spoke her mind about the hideousness of the Bushtucker Trials. I think about her every time I'm eating something awful in a restaurant and I wuss out of complaining and simply smile and say, 'It's lovely!' I loved how Jennie and Vanessa, who are professional performers, were happy to mess about with me and sing for their suppers. Overall, everyone in the jungle showed me how important it is to have a sense of humour about yourself. They made me learn and grow, and ensured I had a fantastic time doing it.

My manager, Gemma

Sometimes I describe Gemma as my 'nanny', and I know my mum loves her, because she's the only person who looks after me almost as well as she does. Maybe Gemma's more like a big sister. She can be quite strict with me – but then, she is the one who has to make sure I don't have too many tequilas when I have a six a.m. alarm call, and that's a full-time job in itself.

Gemma inspires me with her endless patience and the fact that she's committed to making sure that I fulfil my potential. Sometimes, ambition can be a bit embarrassing. Before Gemma was looking after me, I wasn't sure how to talk about what I wanted to do, and I was nervous that people might laugh at me for dreaming big. However, I could call Gemma now and tell her that I dreamed of having my own T.V. show and meeting Oprah, and Gemma would simply say, 'Right. Let's think of a way to make that happen.' Gemma's patience doesn't just extend to hitting redial and getting me out of bed on time. She thinks in the long-term and makes me consider my future goals thoughtfully. She's very good at making me feel as though I can do absolutely anything, while reminding me that I don't have to do it all *today*.

London

I'm not sure that I completely believe in reincarnation, but if I were to die and come back as a bus route, I'd be the number 22. That journey defines me. You simply don't need to go anywhere else. It takes in all of the hotspots.

Jump on at Putney Common or Parsons Green, motor up the King's Road and watch some of the world's sweetest, most spoiled dogs having their daily constitutional, then get to Sloane Square via my spiritual home, Peter Jones. Then you're off to Knightsbridge. It's a bonus if the traffic's bad, because here you can gaze into some of the finest shop windows in the world and spend thousands of imaginary pounds while you wait for the lights to change. Then you sail past a double park pile-up – Hyde and Green – before reaching Berkley Square, which is where singers through the ages have been hearing nightingales, but you're more likely to hear someone in a suit muttering about mergers.

(I'm obsessed with the history of London, and I could give you a very nerdy lesson about Berkley Square. If you've never been, I demand that you get off my bus and have a look. You're not allowed to come back on until you've taken photos of the Alexander Munro fountain and a plane tree. The trees on this square are some of the oldest in London, according to my wisest friends and Wikipedia.)

Then, if you must, you can get back on and go to Oxford Circus, but, frankly, I wouldn't bother. You'll only get hot and cross, which are the worst shopping conditions imaginable. Everything you need is just a few stops south. Peter Jones even sells Liberty-print fabric in the haberdashery department now, so it's possible to experience the highlights of the West End while remaining true to your Sloane soul.

Still, that's not to say I'm closed minded about the city I live in. One of the things that I adore about London is that every day spent in the capital is a school day. It's impossible not to learn new things, even if you're one of those people who keeps their headphones in and their eyes closed, and you travel everywhere by taxi. (Don't, though, if you can avoid it. You can hear the most divine gossip on the bus, if you're a good listener.)

Weirdly, one of the best London facts I learned recently was a piece of information I acquired in the middle of the Australian jungle. I was talking to my dear friend Stanley Johnson, and I was just burbling nonsense. I think we'd finished all of the proper food some time ago and, unless we fancied voluntarily tucking into some worms, we'd be going hungry until morning. I was too hungry even to be hangry! Usually, if I don't have any supper, I become a furious ball of rage, but for some reason I skipped that stage and went straight to the mad rambling. So, poor Stanley was just listening to me chatting rubbish, talking about my favourite places in London, and suddenly I burst out with, 'What on *earth* is that big thing in the middle of Battersea Park?'

Clever Stanley, who was making much more sense than me, said, 'That's not a "thing"! It's called a pagoda, and it was presented to Londoners by the Venerable Nichidatsu Fujii, close mate of Mahatma Gandhi, in 1984.'

I was astonished. How on earth did he know that?

'I remember when it went up. And the fountains nearby were built in 1951, as part of the Festival of Britain. I was around for those, too!' he explained.

This is, I think, one of the very best things about living in London. I have my own special memories, like accidentally drenching Mark-Francis with champagne at Loulou's, and dancing at KOKO in Camden, infiltrating the D.J. booth and blaring my favourite hymn, 'Jerusalem', to the entire club at one o'clock on a Sunday morning. And there was the time when I thought it was a great idea to take a dip in the fountain in the middle of Sloane Square. It wasn't even summer, and I had an extremely soggy walk down the King's Road on my way home. Still, I was triumphant! I'd achieved one of my biggest ambitions, and I'd discovered that the fountain is at least two feet deep. Everyone you meet has their own precious memories, too, and you can learn so much from them. London is constantly changing and shifting, yet, somehow, it's always the same. Almost everyone you meet will have experienced the city differently, and, in London, you can always find common ground.

How I found my way to London

Most people don't realize I'm not actually from Chelsea. In fact, I think they assume that I was born outside Buckingham Palace, wearing one of those bearskin hats and holding a Tube map. Yet, technically, home is Torquay, in Devon. Still, I'm a big believer in the idea that you can have more than one home. I mean, not like James Taylor, with his west London pad and his Yorkshire pile, although that does seem delightful, too. Although, I suppose the tricky thing about straddling multiple postcodes is that you never know where you've left your phone charger. Anyway, I think that you can be born in one part of the world, but find yourself emotionally and spiritually connecting with a completely different bit. One day, you'll arrive in a brand-new city and feel as though you've spent your entire life travelling to get there. You'll wake up and feel as though you've finally arrived, even if you've spent the night on a camp bed in a hall, using your handbag for a pillow. Because that's exactly how I felt when I got to London.

My parents have always described me as having 'an old head on young shoulders', which might be why they let me embrace my inner Dick Whittington when I was sixteen. (If you're thinking of running away to London, here's one piece of important, practical advice: you really can't fit much in a knapsack, and there's nowhere to put an enormous stick during rush hour on the Piccadilly Line. Get a little wheelie case instead.) I'd just finished my GCSEs, and I was desperate to rush off to London for the summer.

At this point, I already knew the city quite well. I'd been spending some sneaky weekends going to parties in west London, visiting my grandparents in Berkshire and using them as a base. Admittedly, I was quite naughty. I didn't really get up to mischief once I'd got to London – I just wanted to go out dancing – but, more than once, I did get to school on Monday morning without having gone to bed. Those early trips were so exciting. I remember queuing up to get into clubs on the King's Road, feeling giddy about the fun I was going to have! The idea of spending the summer in Devon simply didn't appeal, even though some people say it's their favourite holiday destination. They dream of the seaside, ice creams and donkey rides; I dreamed of Hyde Park, fruit and veg stalls and black cabs. I presented the idea to my parents as a fait accompli and, rather wearily, they agreed to let me live with a friend in Elephant and Castle, and work in a shop. That was back when Mahiki Mondays were brilliant and people used to

If you want to bond with a Sloane, simply roll your eyes and say, "I just got stuck on the District Line," and let them enjoy a solid whinge.

queue up around the block. I think I spent some of the happiest times of my life standing outside and looking forward to having a proper Mahiki boogie.

Now, if you don't know London, you might think that Elephant and Castle sounds rather fabulous. If you *do*, you might be surprised that I didn't take one look at it, wrinkle my nose and spend the summer taking tea at Fortnum's instead. I meet plenty of people who think Elephant and Castle is the stuff of nightmares. In fact, I'm pretty sure that my friend Victoria hallucinated that she was trapped there on the Bakerloo Line, after taking some extremely strong pain medication for a toothache. But I adored my time in south-east London. In fact, I still go out there occasionally, I just need to bring the right headgear. It's a part of town that's made for trucker caps, not tiaras.

I had the best summer of my life there. I wasn't earning very much, so every day I'd buy my fruit and veg from the market, right before closing time, to get the best deals. The most amazing woman ran the stall I'd go to, and she also used to make outfits for me to wear when I went out. Sometimes, I'd go back to the flat laden down with tomatoes and cucumbers – and a brand-new dress to wear that night – and making dinner would take a backseat to making plans. I was constantly running around, but London never wore me out. In fact, it seemed to give me even more energy. Towards the end of the summer, I got an early-morning call from my mum.

'Well?' she said.

'Well, what?' I asked, confused. It wasn't quite ten o'clock, I had no idea what she was talking about and I had the beginnings of a headache.

'Your GCSEs! What did you get?'

I had no idea. I'd completely forgotten it was results day.

After a bit of ringing round and post opening, we ascertained that I'd got a clutch of A and A* grades. Mum and Dad were very proud – and, I think, *slightly* irritated that I was the only sixteen-year-old in the country who had actually forgotten to check her results. Honestly, that's London for you: I think it's impossible to worry too much about what might happen, because there's so much to concentrate on in the now. Some people find that being in quiet, tranquil surroundings is what helps them to meditate and stay grounded. For me, London is where I live in the moment. It's too busy and bustling to allow you to do anything else. The present has a universal postcode.

My summer in London made me feel even more confident and certain I belonged there. After finishing my A-levels, it was the only place I could consider going, so I took up my place at the University of Westminster, which was chosen mostly for its location. Like Madonna, I wanted to be in the centre of everything. As you know, university wasn't right for me – but London was. Shortly after moving here, I started to appear on *Made in Chelsea*, which was thrilling. As I've said, I never saw myself going into television, but the idea of being on a programme that was all about London, my favourite place, was irresistible. And it meant meeting people who were just as passionate about the place as I was.

I love exploring new places and I'm incredibly lucky to have had the opportunity to travel all over the world. Still, no matter where I go, I think I'll always come back to London. It's home, and there's nowhere else that I could see myself living.

From the Australian Bush to Shepherd's Bush: Toff's guide to surviving new cities and situations

Be optimistic

Seeing a brand-new place, whether you're there for a visit or it's a permanent move, is going to bring up lots of positive and negative emotions. Hopefully, you'll be excited about the fact that everything seems new and different, but it's normal to feel a bit confused and vulnerable, too. Ultimately, you'll see the new place through your own filter, and you can choose how you view it, even before you arrive. Decide to focus on the good, the different and the surprising. You're an emotional architect and you can build your feelings in order to get the best out of the city.

Take one day at a time

It sounds so obvious, but this was the only way I could survive the jungle. I think that, sometimes, people feel as though they can get through a tricky situation if they stick to a plan and a strategy, but, when you're in a new place, it's difficult to predict what's going to happen. When I arrived in Australia, I had no idea who my closest friends would be, and I didn't know how I was going to react to the witchetty grubs, and I certainly had no useful tactics when it came to sharing the experience with Ant and Dec afterwards. If I'd tried to plan and use techniques, I know I would have become stressed and scared. So, I just went with it and did my best to focus on what was happening at that moment, instead of worrying about what tomorrow would bring. I think that's the best way to survive in any new place. There will be plenty of time to think about tomorrow, when it's tomorrow. The only things that should be worrying you today, should be happening today. Even theatre tickets can be bought on the morning of the show, instead of months in advance. Don't fret because you might get mugged tomorrow. Celebrate because you haven't been mugged today! If you have been mugged today, remember that it's extremely unusual to get mugged two days in a row.

Do your homework – and put your hand up

As you know, I'm always shocking myself by discovering how little I know about London. Then again, in the jungle, Amir Khan didn't know what a gecko was, even when he'd been surrounded by geckos for a fortnight. Every place you go will have a wealth of facts and experiences to offer. You can learn for a lifetime and you still won't be finished. Weirdly, I was in London with my friend and a strange man approached us and started asking us riddles. He said that he loved riddles because solving problems keeps your brain young. I've learned that London will *never* stop surprising me, and that the people you find are just as interesting as the places you visit. Also, that riddles make your brain hurt – I don't know whether that's the same as keeping it young!

Still, it's nice to be informed about something. Be a nerd. Read up on whatever interests you, even if it doesn't seem relevant. For example, it's nice to be able to point out Battersea Power Station. It's even nicer to be able to tell a story about it. Did you know that Pink Floyd attached an inflatable pink pig to one of the towers, to shoot the cover of their *Animals* album? Did you know that the pig then blew away and briefly ended up on the Heathrow airport flight path, confusing several pilots, before landing in a field in Kent? It wouldn't matter if you didn't know what a pigeon was, if you had that thrilling fact up your sleeve. Also, ask questions. Get a local talking about where they live and you'll learn so much. It's always better to admit ignorance and learn than it is to pretend you know everything and stay stupid.

Be a tourist!

Admittedly, I'm biased, because London is probably the very best place to be a tourist in your own town, but sometimes it makes sense to follow the crowd. People are horrible about tourists, but usually they're the ones who are making an effort to seek out the best and most interesting places to go. Sure, they don't always have great taste. (Why do so many tourists seem to love nothing more than hanging out at the interchange at Bank Underground station? Even for a hard-core trainspotter and T.F.L. nerd, there isn't that much to see. Perhaps the kiosk by the ticket barriers does a surprisingly good sausage roll.) However, the tourists are the people who are looking up, slowing down and noticing every single exciting detail about the place they're in. Go to your local gallery. (Or find me in mine, the Saatchi – I've been going with my mum since I was a teenager!) Try a brand-new café, instead of always going to the same pub. See what's growing in your nearest park. We always talk about wanting to fit in straight away and live like a local when we've been in a new place for two days. Don't be embarrassed about being new; you'll have more fun and be much more enthusiastic if you embrace your tourist tendencies. Also, this means you'll have more opportunities for souvenir shopping!

Don't compare home and away

When I'm in a new place, one of my worst habits is to look for familiar things. I've been in Paris, city of light, love and art, and got ridiculously overexcited after spotting a McDonald's! I think it's natural to do this, up to a point, but when you're new and experiencing something for the first time, it's a shame to try to see it in the context of what you already know. You're dealing with the unknown. That's the point. Going to London and moaning about the price of a pint and the crowds and queues is a bit like going to Devon and complaining about the fact that it's close to the sea and that all of the fields have cows in them. Let go of what you know and focus on finding the fun in the new and exciting.

Get a table for one

This is one of my very favourite things to do. As much as I adore company and a good lunch or dinner gossip with one of my best friends, I think that the greatest way to take in a new place is to treat yourself to some solo dining. Admittedly, this one wasn't really so easy to do in the jungle. Imagine if I'd said, 'Sorry, I need to be alone with my blended pig's brain,' and sneaked off into a leafy corner for some Toff time! I guess, that way, I wouldn't have felt quite so embarrassed about the faces I was making. Anyway, let's assume you're exploring a place with cafes and restaurants, and wildlife is off the menu. Try to find somewhere fairly busy, because you're after gossip and buzz. After all, you don't know what – or who – you might see, and where they might lead you! If you can eat while sitting at the bar, you're brilliantly placed to listen out for chat, stories and interesting information. Also, most bar staff are usually up for a bit of a gossip. Get them talking and they'll fill you in on what's happening and help you to discover where you should go next. (Do tip lavishly – the chat is always worth it!) Eating by yourself is one of the best ways to learn all about your new environment, as well as having a considerable advantage if you're greedy, like me. You can order and eat two puddings, and no one else will be able to judge you for doing so.

Some rules for living

The trouble with modern life is that we don't always get to choose where we live, or even who we live with, and most of us might find ourselves making a few tiny compromises here and there on our paths to domestic bliss. I've always been incredibly lucky with my housemates, and I've never had a bad one yet. That said, there's a rule of thumb that can be applied in any group situation, whether it's an orgy or in a box at the opera. There's always going to be one dickhead in the gang and, if you can't immediately identify them, the dickhead is probably you. I know that sounds quite alarming, but don't worry. On occasion, we're all absolutely terrible; it's just an unavoidable part of the human condition. However, it's worth keeping an eye on your dickhead tendencies and making sure that they're not having an enormous impact on the people you live with – whether they're your parents, your friends, some people you found on the Internet, or, in case of some of my fanciest friends, your staff. For starters, if you're in a house-share that has gone nightmarishly wrong, you need to be able to retain the moral high ground. If you're raising an issue with a heinous housemate, you don't want them to respond by pointing at you and saying, 'Takes one to know one!'

I've always been very independent, partly because I was at boarding school when I was a teenager, so I only came home at weekends – and, even then, I spent more time queuing at ticket barriers at Paddington and Waterloo than skulking in my room and leaving a trail of unwashed cereal bowls and wet towels in my wake (every parent's top source of exasperation). But I know plenty of people who live at home with their parents, at least some of the time. If you get on well with your mum and dad, it's a brilliant idea. There are no surprises, hopefully you'll have a bit of space, and parents tend to be much better than their children at stocking the fridge and paying the electricity bill. The other day, a friend came over and I could offer her seven different kinds of tea, but no milk. My mum simply wouldn't let this happen – and her store cupboard contains enough biscuits for the whole family to survive the first five years of a nuclear war. Anyway, there's a reason why parents occasionally resort to the old cliché about how their grown-up children treat their house like a hotel – and it's because the sheets have a higher thread count than ours, the bathroom has nicer toiletries and the breakfast is included. You don't have to think about anything – parents will do your thinking for you. It's a lovely, relaxing holiday for the mind, but it can be deeply dangerous.

The difficulty with living with your parents once you're out of your teens is that you need to negotiate a brand-new relationship with them, otherwise you'll all revert to type and make each other miserable. In my experience, the most dangerous time to move back home is after university. I know people who have been rubbish at the most basic domestic chores – they can't do their laundry without setting their socks on fire – so they go home, where their bed is made for them, literally and figuratively, and they don't make themselves learn. I might not have finished uni, but I learned *quite quickly* that cooking and cleaning aren't optional extras, and that loo roll does not magically appear next to the toilet when you need it.

So, even if you are living with your parents, you need to make sure they treat you like a grown-up – by behaving like one. Imagine that you were involved in some kind of house swap, and you were a guest of your parents' friends. Or that you'd gone online and found a couple of people to live with, who just happened to prefer Radio 3 and the White Company catalogue to Snapchat and a trip to the Camden Assembly. You'd be on your best behaviour! You certainly wouldn't stomp out of the shower, drip all over the kitchen floor and complain that no one had replaced the Cocoa Pops.

Not that I've always been a perfect flatmate. When I shared a flat with my best friends, Jess and Emily, the worst thing I did was stealing food. I'd always replace it, but I was really awful about sneaking cheese. I'd nick slivers of cheddar here and there, and Jess would get *furious*. I can't blame her. When you're a bit hungover, you've come home from a long day and someone has come between you and your cheese on toast, you're bound to get cross. Jess would yell, 'Toff! WHY? WHY DO YOU ALWAYS DO THIS? I KEEP TELLING YOU NOT TO DO THIS!' But she'd get her own back by leaving her old teabags in the sink, which I think is the most revolting thing ever. Then we'd make up in bed! We used to hang out in her room, snuggled up on the pillows, listening to music. Jess has the coolest music collection, which more than made up for the teabag trouble.

In many ways, living with your parents is much easier than having traditional housemates, because it's easier to exploit the dynamic of being their child who needs looking after, even if you're a thirty-two-year-old fund manager. Traditional housemates will not cut you slack, or tidy up after you, unless you're poorly and your arms have actually fallen off. Traditional housemates will leave you furious notes exclaiming that they bought the last four bottles of washing-up liquid, and everyone now owes them

38p. Traditional housemates will also forget to set up a direct debit for the broadband, ensuring your Internet drops out right in the middle of a really good Princess Margaret tantrum on *The Crown*. Traditional housemates will have sex, quite loudly and drunkenly, at four o'clock in the morning, when you've got to leave for work in two hours. They will borrow the vintage dress that used to belong to your godmother, and then lend it to a drag queen, who immediately takes it on tour to Amsterdam, decides to move there and posts Instagram pictures of themselves wearing it, while refusing to respond to your urgent messages. Yet, housemates are the best. Living in a good house-share is like being in the throes of a mad and furious love affair, and you'll have moments when you think that there's nowhere you'd rather be than in your sitting room, wrapped in a duvet, dissecting the night before. One day, you will leave and find a home of your own. There will be moments when you'll wonder how you and your crockery survived the house-share, but, with any luck, you'll look back and think of it as one of the best things you've ever done.

I loved living with my best friends – Emily, Jess and Lottie. It was a really happy time, although our flat was literally a madhouse. You know when you go to a big supermarket at the weekend, and you see a gang of little kids who are out of their mind on Smarties, racing each other up and down the aisles on trolleys? That was our constant energy level.

Sharing a flat with your favourite people is heaven, but the stakes are very high. Marilyn Monroe is thought to have once said, 'If you can't handle me at my worst, then you sure as hell don't deserve me at my best.' While that's an extremely obnoxious thing to say, I do sometimes wonder whether she first thought of it during an inter-flatmate screaming match, while someone was shouting at her for nicking their hairdryer. When you decide to live with friends, you know everything there is about their best qualities, and you could go on *Mastermind* with their lovability and general brilliance as your specialist subject. However, after three months of gritty floors, dirty mugs, piled-up post and friends of their friends coming all the way from New Zealand to live on your uncomfy two-seater sofa, something is going to snap.

Chances are that you will look back at it all one day and laugh, but do remember that the wrong house-share can undo the very best friendship. I think ours worked because we had a perfect mix of personalities, and we were all great communicators who could respect each other's space. OK, I'll admit the truth. We all survived the experience because we got a cleaner. Let's be honest: everyone hates housework. Even if you start off liking it, if you feel as though you're the person who does everything, you'll go off it in about half an hour. Also, when the subject is debated (read: argued about), everybody has a mysterious belief that they're the one who is constantly on their hands and knees, scrubbing, while all of the other housemates lie on the sofa, making mounds of toast crumbs. It's like one of those old-fashioned maths textbook questions: *If the housemates, between them, claim to be doing three hundred hours of housework a week, yet the bin is a health hazard and no one can see the floor, who is telling the biggest lie?* If you get a cleaner, you can't argue about who is contributing

71

> **If I were to die and come back as a bus route, I'd be the number 22.**

the most or least, because the cost is split equally between you. Most importantly, the house can't get too unbearably revolting, as long as it's being cleaned once a week.

This brings me to a relatively new phenomenon: living with people you don't know very well. London, especially, is a fast-moving city. While most of us might hope that our adult living arrangements will be a cross between student halls and Monica's apartment in *Friends*, it's not necessarily that easy. You'll be happy in your flat-share, and then someone will suddenly announce they're moving to Tokyo, and someone else will move out to live with their boyfriend, and someone else will break up – it's like playing musical chairs in the middle of Ikea. Occasionally, the music will stop and you won't be able to live with whomever you like. You'll be forced to throw yourself on the mercy of people you don't know that well, and hope it works out. Luckily for me, it always has.

Before I shared a flat with the girls, I lived with a lovely couple called Alex and Hermione. They were proper grown-ups, which meant that I had to behave like one, too – mainly by not waking them up after I came back from a night out, which I think I managed at least sixty per cent of the time. Because I didn't know them that well, I couldn't take them for granted, and I always tried to be super respectful of the fact that they were sharing their home with me. Also, my rent was very cheap, partly because I was sleeping on a bed that had been wedged into an airing cupboard. It was pretty big, as airing cupboards go, but you couldn't ignore the fact that the space had been designed for towels, not Toffs. Still, I was incredibly happy in my cupboard, and I'm so glad I lived there before moving in with the girls. It was a bit like going to housemate school, and it gave me a chance to learn about living with people before I tried it with my best friends.

When you live with people you already love, you're placing pressure on the relationship, but when you live with people who are new to you, you'll probably discover some fabulous friends. If you've just moved to a new city, it might be your only option, but it's also the best way to build your own social network. If it doesn't work out, you can always move house. It's annoying, but it's much, much easier than looking for a new best friend, which sometimes has to happen when a flat-share goes wrong. I mean, if you're going to stop talking to your favourite person, you need to do so for reasons of passion, drama and intrigue – a love affair gone wrong, a priceless heirloom stolen, a significant betrayal. You don't want to have to tell everyone that you and your best bud are no longer speaking because one of you accidentally ate the other one's *butter*.

I think my domestic odyssey has ended now that I have my own place. It's tiny, and it's mine. I can smother myself in fake tan and no one cares about my smell. I can smoke out of the window, although this would be a terrible thing to do and obviously I would never consider it – it's extremely naughty and it would mean that I wouldn't get my deposit back. I can spread out on the sofa and make unilateral decisions about candles and cushions. Most importantly, I can leave half a pizza in the fridge at night, and the next time I open the fridge, *the pizza will still be there*. It's magical. Before I moved in, I wondered whether I might be lonely, but I was quite excited about spending some time by myself. I thought it would mark the beginning of a brand-new, grown-up, mature chapter in my life, filled with quiet contemplation. That was before I realized that, if you live in the middle of Chelsea, your friends will be on your doorstep more frequently than the milkman. The bell goes constantly. I can't hear myself think! Quiet contemplation, indeed . . . If I want some of that, I have to go *out*.

Come for supper!

You've probably guessed that there's a fairly obvious reason I picked Chelsea as my home: the parties. Chelsea is party central. In SW3, more parties are being planned, discussed and analysed at any given second than during an entire night of election broadcasting. Two people out together and drinking wine makes a date – but three inevitably leads to a party. South-west London is to fun what Wembley is to enormous crowds of drunk people paying upwards of £50 to scream inside a giant, sweaty stadium.

The trouble comes when you realize that fun is finite, and you can only get out what you put in. Or rather, being a guest is the best, but your friends are going to get incredibly grumpy when it occurs to them that they have hosted you four times in a row and all they've had from you for their trouble is a few bunches of flowers and half a bag of Kettle Chips, which you opened in the taxi to theirs because you got hungry. You need to send out some invitations before you stop getting invited anywhere.

Unless you happen to own your own restaurant, or you're an heir to a bitcoin fortune, the first problem you face as a host is where you're going to put everyone. For me, some nights it's a struggle to make enough room in my flat to feed myself. This is one of the reasons that I go out so much. There's barely enough space for *me* in the apartment, and I'm tiny! However, there are ways of dealing with this.

You could propose a yoga theme, and force your guests to eat dinner while standing on one leg, with the other leg draped around someone else's neck. This will save on space, although it gets quite messy when dinner is served, invariably ending with someone spilling guacamole on the curtains.

You could tell everyone that you've just been burgled by a petty criminal who took all of your cushions, and every sitting surface is still being investigated by forensics, so no one is allowed to sit down. Hopefully, this will distract everyone from the fact that there isn't really enough room for them and you only have two chairs. However, you will spend the evening making up more lies about the cushion burglar and will get so immersed in the story that you'll probably forget to take anything out of the oven, the smoke alarm will go off, the building will be evacuated and your landlord will get seriously grumpy.

So, the best way to deal with the London lack-of-space issue is to be upfront, honest – and to exaggerate. Tell everyone that you're having a party and you'd love them to come, but your place is so tiny that it's effectively a dolls' house. Tell them you can only bathe by climbing into the sink, and you use the kitchen blinds as a towel. Tell them that the Official Historical Society of Borrowers wants to put a blue plaque by your front door – only, the door is so tiny that it would be concealed entirely by the plaque, and they are forming a resizing committee. Tell them that, when you order pizza, you've been tempted to recycle the box and use it as a carpet because it takes up all of your floor space. Then, when your friends do visit, they will gasp in astonishment because they've been preparing themselves for the worst and, compared with what was going on in their imagination, you live in a palatial mansion.

Now, you need to work out what to serve them. Don't worry! No one ever comes to a dinner party because they suspect you secretly have a Michelin star, but were far too modest to say. Mostly, they want to see you, because they love you, and to get very drunk. Now, my most etiquette-obsessed friends (Hello, Mark!) would say not to bring wine to a dinner party because it becomes madly complicated. You know how there are weird rules about international manners, and that, in some countries, burping after eating is a huge compliment, but if you were to say, 'Thank you, that was lovely,' your host would be expected to take you out into the back garden and shoot you? Well, according to the poshest people, wine is an absolute minefield of manners doom. Smart people assume that their hosts will already have a cellar full of fine claret, and the exact contents should be kept as private as a knicker drawer. In fact, they believe that turning up with a perfectly drinkable bottle of £8 Rioja is tantamount to standing on someone's doorstep, waving a hot pink, frilly nylon thong, shouting, 'I saw this and thought of you!'

However, if I were to invite you to come for dinner, I'd be delighted if you turned up with £8 Rioja – or some Rioja that you won in a raffle. In fact, the only time it's acceptable to come without wine is if you're supposed to be doing Dry January or Sober October. (In this instance, we all know that you'll get halfway through a very boring glass of fizzy elderflower nonsense before looking longingly at the booze and saying, 'Maybe just the one.') One day, I hope to live in a house with a claret cellar, and I shall invite you all over to drink it with me. But, if you're under thirty, it's perfectly OK to ask your guests to bring a bottle.

Catering-wise, the best place to start is with crisps. Who doesn't love a delicious crisp? Tasty, absorbent and available in flavours to suit the fussiest eater, a crisp can be wheat- and dairy-free, vegan, organic – and still be something that hungry people want to eat. Dips and vegetables will make proceedings feel sophisticated, but they are mainly there for decorative reasons. Do not do anything mad like spending an entire afternoon trying to make your own hummus. The effort-to-reward ratio is worse than trying to get the last bit of hand cream out of the bottom of a tube. The same for bowls of olives. Some people like them; most people will put their cigarettes out in them.

Personally, I'm a pretty good chef. I like cooking for myself when I have time – and when I've locked myself out of my

Deliveroo account. However, dinner parties aren't just about cooking – they're about terrifying, impenetrable levels of maths. Richard, my cleverest friend, knows how to build robots, and he'd rather take everyone out for dinner than work out how much pasta you need to feed eight people. Also, most recipes are rubbish, because the quantities might say it's for six or for four, but that's assuming every person will want to eat exactly the same amount of food. I need a recipe that says, *Feeds one friend who is ravenous because they've just come off a juice fast, two who have the most horrible hangovers they have ever known and have been mainlining carbs all day, and one who is heartbroken and will deliver a lengthy, tragic monologue about her loveless state to every single potato she spears with a fork.*

Then, there's the maths of timing, which is worse. How are people supposed to cook entire meals for several people without getting distracted, popping out for a cigarette, ringing someone for a chat and then coming back two hours later to discover that their house is full of firemen? Well, actually, that sounds like a bit of a bonus . . .

If you would like to try cooking, but you're stuck for ideas, just do a roast. I've never met anyone who isn't excited about having a roast dinner, especially when it's not Sunday. The novelty factor is strong. The vegetarians can just eat roast potatoes, and the recipe for those is extremely easy. Simply peel potatoes until you feel as though your arms are going to fall off, then cut them up, boil them for a bit and put them in the oven with lots of salt and olive oil. Some people will say that you must use goose fat or duck fat for crispiness and flavour. To them, I say, 'Clearly, you've never had to comfort a weeping vegan after she just found out that she accidentally ate some goose.'

If you spend the week before the dinner party waking up in the night, drenched in a cold sweat, fresh from a nightmare that you've shut down an entire wing of St Mary's hospital by giving all of your best friends gastroenteritis, don't bother cooking. It's perfectly acceptable to get someone else to do the catering for you – even the Colonel, Ronald McDonald or the Little Chef. (Definitely offer a lollipop to the first person to clean their plate; dinners go well when there's a competitive element.)

Ultimately, don't worry too much. London is full of amazing restaurants and, if people are fussy about their food, I'd say they can just go to one of those instead of coming to my house for their dinner. I can certainly promise my guests a memorable meal. It might not exactly be award-winning cuisine, but I can guarantee they'll be talking about it for years to come.

The sillier and scruffier your dinner party, the jollier your guests will be. If you go to the trouble of hosting something incredibly elaborate, your guests will become spoiled, obnoxious and embarrassing. Give someone half a pizza and a pint glass half filled with Blossom Hill rosé, and they will act like a grown-up. Put them in a grand room, give them fabulous food prepared by someone else, limitless booze, fresh flowers and a theme, and they'll act like a bigger baby than George Dawes in *Shooting Stars*. I don't know what it is about a well-drizzled *jus* that drives people to start screaming across a table, but if you're hosting a lavish dinner party, you'll need to know how to break up a fight between your guests.

Firstly, never underestimate the power of distraction. If you've been waiting to drop a sizzling gossip bomb, deploy it immediately. Nothing *too* inflammatory – and now I'm mixing metaphors; bombs are inherently inflammatory – but, essentially, you don't want your bit of distraction to start another fight at the other end of the table. An engagement or a pregnancy will take the heat off and redirect the negative energy, and you can always massage the truth a bit. For example, 'Oh, sorry, I *thought* I might be engaged, but I just put my ring on the wrong hand.'

If you want to stop your guests from getting into mischief and shouting at each other, serve them lobsters! Unfortunately, I learned this by accident. On *Come Dine With Me*, I thought that it would be fun to serve lobsters to Jamie, Mytton and Louise! Everyone loves lobsters, right?! In fact, I ordered them and persuaded the fishmonger to cook them for me, so it should have been foolproof. Yet, when I served them up, I realized that I couldn't offer anyone anything to open the lobsters with, so I got some hammers from the attic. Jamie almost broke the dinner table with his hammering and there's *still* lobster on the ceiling. It's in my old flat – I actually had to move house to get away from my embarrassing, stinky mistake! Still, everyone bonded with each other pretty sharpish – we were united in hilarity. None of us will ever forget lobster-ceiling night.

Celebrity friends are useful for creating a distraction, especially ones who have a helicopter and a lot of free time. This is a rare combination – you might as well try to find a goat who is doing the 5:2 – but, ideally, you need someone who is impressive, available and bound to be more exciting than any fight that might be going on, so you can stand on your chair and say, 'Oh, look, look! Everyone go outside – I think Kanye might be landing on the lawn.' If this is a struggle, lay some groundwork. Try to imply you have celebrity friends, with a few unsubtle, laboured mentions. For example, if you see someone drinking a Nespresso, say, 'Oh, my friend *George* likes that coffee.' Or, when watching a police procedural drama, say, 'I could see my friend *George* in something like this, and he's married to a lawyer, too!' Then, when the fighting begins, get everyone to shut up by telling them *George* is coming. They will be distracted by anticipation, and then by their own disappointment when they discover your mate is just a chap named George. In my case, they're especially upset when the George that turns up is George Osborne.

Seating plans are invariably awful at a Chelsea dinner, because everyone who was friends when you planned the party will have fallen out over some triviality by the time the canapés are being served. It's worse than a wedding, on steroids. So, I say, don't bother. If you like place cards and those little maps that tell you where everyone is supposed to sit, make it a mystery. Just don't bother putting any useful information on them. Everyone will constantly be moving around, anyway. If anyone complains about the lack of placement, simply shrug and say, 'It's organic.'

How to know if someone really is 'Chelsea' – spotting an SW socialite from sixty paces

I reckon I know as much about south-west Londoners as David Attenborough knows about whales. In fact, possibly slightly more, because I have a native's advantage. David Attenborough is, after all, a man of considerable skills and talents, but he is not an actual whale. Ever since I arrived in London seven years ago, I've been studying my tribe and familiarizing myself with the habits, characteristics and ways of living that define us. Here are the behaviours that make up the quintessential west Londoner.

We're always 'nipping' down the King's Road

There is only one mode of transportation when it comes to travelling up and down Chelsea's most significant street, and that is the 'nip'. You can't walk or run down the road, but I suppose you could pop or dash, at an absolute push. I nip down the King's Road at least once a day, because I'm always running out of something essential that can only be purchased from Peter Jones or the Saatchi Gallery.

Chelsea dwellers are constantly in a state of fury about the slowness of the District Line

I promise you that you could go to Dubai and hear people complaining about the District Line. You could be at a Royal Garden Party and, if the Queen asked you whether you had far to come, you might say, 'Well, technically, Your Majesty, I should have been here in ten minutes, this is right around the corner from me, but it was a *nightmare* because of the sodding District Line! I spent half an hour sweating on the platform at Earl's Court! I nearly sacked off your do and tried to go home on the Piccadilly Line!' If you want to bond with a Sloane, simply roll your eyes and say, 'I just got stuck on the District Line,' and let them enjoy a solid whinge.

One day, we'll go for a picnic

Richmond Park is on our doorstep, and it's *beautiful*. We have deer there. Nothing could be nicer than gathering a hamper, loading yourself up with all of the rosé you can carry, jumping on the Tube and meeting your friends for a picnic on a hot summer's day. Yet, to the best of my knowledge, no one has ever managed to achieve this simple goal. This will probably be my eighth London summer of talking at length about a Richmond Park picnic, and failing to go. To be honest, at this stage, no picnic could possibly live up to these heightened expectations. If you've managed a Magnum on the benches in Sloane Square, you're doing better than most of us.

When we drink, we need to give everything a ridiculous name

We don't just have our own special beer – the Chelsea Blonde – we drink it in a pub called the Sloaney Pony. OK, so, the pub is *really* called the White Horse, but you can't live in south-west London unless you're prepared to take the piss out of yourself. Drinking in Chelsea is a simultaneously serious and extremely silly affair. I believe that we have the jolliest pubs in London, and we're completely committed to the pursuit of pleasure, which is why our watering holes have the comfiest seats and best selection of crisps. Also, the best way to spot a spiritual south-west Londoner is to check someone's willingness to share their salty snacks. If you crack open the entire bag and spread it out on the table, you're one of us. If you keep your crisps to yourself without offering them around, we won't invite you back.

We're labouring under the misapprehension that we live in the country

I think one of the most hilarious things about us is that we're all pretending we're stuck in some tiny village in a tucked-away corner of Suffolk. Everyone drives cars designed to pull horses out of muddy ditches, when the biggest driving drama we'll ever have to face is an unexpected reverse around a corner after missing the entrance for the Waitrose car park. We wear tweed, gilets, Barbour and big long boots, when the coldest conditions that most of us have to face involve dealing with chilly air con in the back of a black cab. We all adore festivals, because we see them as a chance to be 'at one with nature', even though there is nothing natural about eating a reheated burrito while queuing for a Portaloo at the back of Hyde Park. To be fair, travelling to south-west London takes absolutely ages, and we are quite remote. On a bad day, if you come from Waterloo, it's actually quicker to get to Hampshire.

We're surprisingly resourceful

It's very easy to write off a south-west Londoner and say we don't have many special skills. I can see where our critics are coming from. We live in the land of million-pound houses, lattes that can cost as much as the minimum hourly wage, and Harrods. Chelsea does look like a lovely luxury fairyland where no one's feet touch the ground unless they're getting out of an Addison Lee. However, we've evolved to have a range of special abilities. I think we're some of the friendliest people in London, because we've all grown up to believe that nothing is more vulgar than bad manners, and we're always trying to put people at their ease. I truly believe you could dump us all in the desert and, within an hour, we would have found a source of gin and tonic. A true Chelsea girl would make a dress by wrapping herself in her own curtains before complaining that she had nothing to wear, and she'd go out dancing in it. Also, we never get lost because we always instinctively know that we're heading west.

Going Out

In a way, I wish I could tell you that I'm one of those really cosy girls who loves nothing more than changing into a pair of clean cashmere pyjamas by eight p.m.

I know that staying in is the new going out, that meditating is much more fashionable than Malibu and Coke, and that, if you've gone to all the trouble of learning how to pronounce *hygge*, you probably feel as though you owe it to yourself to invest in a posh blanket and a couple of scented candles. However, I firmly believe that the best thing you can ever do is be true to yourself, even if it means that you're flying in the face of public opinion, style and sense. So, here is my truth: I adore nothing more than a good night out. I was born to party. If it's the weekend and I'm in bed, asleep when the sun comes up, I'm probably somewhere like Iceland, where the sun doesn't rise until lunchtime.

Sure, I have the best intentions. The other day, I decided that I really needed to rest and recuperate, as I had a busy time coming up, and work, and I needed to be refreshed and raring to go. I made myself a herbal tea, I put on my favourite film, *Notting Hill*, and I even put cashmere pyjamas on! I was congratulating myself on being healthy, sensible and grown-up, when the doorbell went. It was Sam and Alex from *Made in Chelsea*, giggling like carol singers who had got the date wrong. Only, instead of launching into 'Good King Wenceslas', their song went, 'Toff-eeeeeee! Come out? Just the one?' Did I tell them to bugger off and let a girl get her beauty sleep? Well, I *tried* – but, before I knew it, we were in a black cab and my pyjamas had mysteriously turned into something sequinned. I felt like Cinderella, kidnapped by a pair of party-loving fairy godfathers, only I had no adorably dressed mouse pals. I didn't even get to meet a handsome prince – just Sam Prince!

Of course, I didn't wake up wishing I'd told the boys to leave me alone, and I didn't wish I'd simply stayed in and had a quiet night. The night may have got *slightly* out of hand (we didn't go out for just the one drink; we didn't even stay in just the one bar, or stop for just the one helping of cheesy chips on the way home), but I knew I'd had fun with my friends and spent a whole night feeling happy and carefree – something more precious and refreshing than an entire crate of champagne.

I know some people who find nights out really stressful. I mean, in Chelsea, a typical party features more drama than every single production the Royal Shakespeare Company has ever performed, watched back-to-back on DVD, with extras and commentary.

Sometimes, people prepare as though they're going into battle, worrying about who they will see, how they'll confront them and pressuring everyone else to take so many sides that we're all in danger of becoming octagonal. This is *mad*, not least because all of this ridiculousness is usually forgotten about in a week. (There are a couple of exceptions, which I will tell you about, but dealing with them can be done with class and style, and ideally *not* when the music goes quiet and everyone is staring at you.)

All you need to have a great night out is a great attitude. There is a time and a place for taking the photo that launched a thousand Instagram likes, or drenching a poisonous ex with a well-timed glass of red wine, or letting your best friend know that her boyfriend is a baddy. But, if you go out with a horrible agenda, you'll have a horrible time. Clubs and bars are sacred temples to joy – a night out really is the time to put all of your worries and cares behind you and follow the fun. Remember, you can't have an argument with anyone when you're dancing on a table. Unless the table is a priceless antique and the owner is threatening to kick you out of their house. In that case, it's time to get down. Here's everything I know about going out. Follow these simple rules and, I promise, you'll have the best time ever.

'Just the one' are the magic words

This is a strange and spooky riddle, and I've never been able to get my head around it. I really think that the scientists at the Royal Society should take this phenomenon very seriously and spend some time studying it. When you've been planning a massive night out for ages, you've booked a blow-dry, bought a new outfit, organized taxis and pre-drinks and tables and an after-party, your night usually stops before it starts. Expectations are sky high, everyone is excited, and then, by eleven, everyone is fiddling with their phones, checking taxi apps, or sending naughty messages to old flames, asking if they're 'still up'. (Of *course* they're still up; the whole world is awake!)

This early end to the evening might have something to do with the fact that at least half of your group started getting ready at three p.m. with a big glass of wine in the bath, and they were looking slightly too tipsy before you got to the first bar. Also, I think it's connected with my earlier theory. The more time you have to plan a night out, the easier it is to turn up with a hidden agenda and, instead of concentrating on having a lovely time, you find yourself obsessively plotting to make your terrible ex fall in love with you all over again and demand your hand in marriage. Benjamin Franklin may have said, 'Fail to prepare, and you prepare to fail,' but I say, 'Leave it to chance, and have a good dance.'

Here's the other part of the conundrum. It's the best bit. Say you've gone to the pub for a Sunday roast and maybe half a mind to watch the rugby. You're slightly hungover from the night before and slightly disappointed because you spent your big Saturday night helping your poorly friend, who has a fondness for those terrible tequila shots that taste like Calpol. You're wearing jeans and a vest under a big jumper, and you've not bothered with any make-up beyond concealer. You might not have remembered to put deodorant on.

Nine hours later, you will still be up, jumper wrapped around your waist, bouncing up and down and singing in a D.J. booth, while your friend says, 'My boss will never believe that I could have food poisoning on two Mondays in a row.'

If you want to have the best night of your life, stick your jeans on and WhatsApp your favourite people, saying, *Pub? I can't stay out too late. We'll have to make it just the one.*

> ❛ What happens in the club stays in the club, and cool girls don't need the Internet to tell them they're having a brilliant time. ❜

Never spend more than half an hour getting ready

This is connected with the 'Just The One' (JTO) principle. I'm a big believer in doing whatever it takes to make yourself feel amazing. If you feel like the best and most confident version of yourself with hair extensions, a teeth-bleaching session and a fully laced, original Victorian corset, then treat yourself to all of those things and go out into the night feeling your absolute best. However, I'm convinced that no one really needs more than thirty minutes to get ready. Sure, if you're having a big, formal dinner or a work event where you know everyone will be taking lots of photographs, you might want to push the boat out and take your time to get dressed and ready to go. Let's be honest, though – those are special occasions, not proper nights out. For a proper night out, you're going to be sweating, jumping, running around and spilling the odd drink. Unless you love to look like the old-school rock act, Kiss, and having mascara on your chin is your style signature, less really is more. Before you leave the house, I think it helps to pick one beauty essential that makes you feel good, get that right, and then give yourself ten minutes to sort out the rest. All I need is my concealer, some fake tan, and I'm out the door. Also, they really should make fast fake-tanning into an Olympic event; I'd get the gold, for sure. Remember, you'll always look gorgeous as long as you're having a good time – and most bars are really dark.

No one can dance in heels (and test your dress)

Ladies, what I'm about to say might shock you, but we need to get real about heels. I grew up believing they were the last word in grown-up glamour. At school, my friends and I were obsessed with adding an extra few inches. Some of us would smuggle heels to parties, hoping our parents wouldn't notice that we seemed to grow about a foot taller every Saturday night and then shrink down again – a bit like Alice in Wonderland, had she purchased her magic potions at Superdry. All I can remember from those parties is that, for the first two hours, everyone looked miserable, as though their lips were as sour as lemons, and no one danced. Then a pile of shoes would start to grow in the middle of the room, as everyone kicked them off, grinned with relief and started tearing it up.

Heels are a horrible conspiracy. Most men don't wear them, and I think that's a big giveaway. Most of the time-consuming, annoying and downright painful parts of looking good are things that men don't feel the need to subject themselves to – even though they're quite fond of the good bits, like massages. If you want to feel grumpy and end the night barefoot, wear heels. If you want to dance until dawn and beyond, while still being able to feel your toes, pack your trainers. Also, you might want to road-test your dress to make sure you can move in it. I've seen plenty of friends laid low by devastatingly sexy bodycon, simply because it's impossible to swing your hips in a skintight dress and you have to spend the night sort of stretched out and propped in a corner, like a Hoover that someone has forgotten to put back in the cupboard.

It's a marathon, not a sprint – and you'll need a kit bag

Every year, I watch the London Marathon and get quite excited when the runners reveal what's in their special kit. They bring everything with them, from spare socks to special energy gels, and I think they must be brilliant at partying, because they're so well prepared – you need exactly the same stuff. I don't like to take a big bag out with me, but, as well as bringing the essentials – card, keys and concealer – I like to take a packet of nuts. They're small, easy to eat, and you can get them out on the dance floor and keep going when it's midnight, you're starving and you can't persuade anyone to bring you chips. It took me a long time to learn how to get this right. I was the laughing stock of London when I first moved here, because I used to carry a wheel of Camembert in my handbag. Frankly, I think people were just epically jealous – there is never a bad time to tuck into some delicious cheese. Still, it's a bit smelly and antisocial, but no one can kick up a stink about some nuts.

The scruffier the club, the more special the night

As someone who is completely committed to fun, I've danced the night away in some of the poshest places in the world. I've dabbed in Dubai, slut-dropped in San Antonio, grinded in Gstaad – or should that be ground? Prince Harry might know. Anyway, I've been in enough V.I.P. areas to know that the most fun is had in the clubs that don't have a V.I.P. area, just a patio with an extractor fan, where the smokers go. This is why I adore my beloved 151 Club. They don't really have a D.J. as such, just an iPhone jack. I've wandered into the kitchen and made myself sandwiches. If the worst happens and I can't get a taxi, I can just about walk home to my front door. (Thanks, trainers!) Everyone else tells me it's the very worst club in London. Everyone else also regularly turns up there at two o'clock in the morning. Sometimes, in yoga classes, the instructor asks us to lie down, close our eyes and think of our happy place. While everyone else is picturing tranquil forests or sandy beaches, I'm imagining myself at the 151 Club, playing 'Saturday Night' and munching a BLT . . .

Dancing > everything else

Look, there's a serious side to all of this fun, and that means getting your priorities in order and approaching the night accordingly. As far as I'm concerned, if you're not dancing, you're not doing it right. Going to the loo for a quick wee is acceptable. Going for a lengthy gossip, trying on three different lipsticks and having a therapy session with the attendant is not on. Similarly, bar queues can't be helped, but if you're in the line for a long time, you might want to think about buying yourself two drinks, so you don't waste your night waiting for white wine. As someone who has spent some time on both sides of the bar, I'd recommend bringing cash out with you, simply because it's speedier than using a card. And if, like me, you have a tendency to lose bags and leave trails of your belongings behind you, like a hedonistic Hansel and Gretel, consider using a bum bag. I might be the only person who thinks the bum bag is a legitimate fashion item, but they're much easier to dance in and harder to lose than something with a fiddly strap.

Put that phone away

Most of the time, I'm as addicted to my iPhone as any other twenty-three-year-old. I'm not proud of this, but at least once a day I'll freak out and scream, 'WHERE'S MY PHONE?' – only to realize it's nestled snugly in the palm of my hand. Phones are fabulous. I don't know where you'd be without yours, but without mine I'd probably be sitting on a pavement crying, two streets away from my flat, convinced I was horribly lost. But nothing good happens when you get your phone out after midnight.

All social-media activity relating to the night out should be over before you leave the first bar. By all means, take a sexy selfie, tag your squad and let your followers know that you're on the brink of having the very best night out of your life. Then zip it into a pocket, turn it off, if you must, and leave it be. If you're worried about capturing your night, your heart isn't in it. More seriously, it simply isn't fair on anyone else. I've lost count of the number of times I've gone for JTO and have found myself in big trouble because I've been tagged with a tableful of shots at two a.m. – and the picture has been liked by the person I have a meeting with at ten a.m. What happens in the club stays in the club, and cool girls don't need the Internet to tell them they're having a brilliant time. They know.

> We'll never lie on our deathbeds and wish we'd had less champagne.

Also, if you have a troubling tendency to text when drunk, a phone ban stops you from doing anything you might regret. Nothing is quite so sobering as seeing your own sweaty face staring back at you from a switched-off phone screen – many's the time that trick has stopped me from messaging a boy with bad intentions.

Befriending and badgering the D.J.

D.J.s work incredibly hard to produce set lists that the crowd will love. They read the room, they entertain us for hours and they're stuck by themselves in their little booth with their headphones on, when everyone knows it's much more fun on the dance floor. I almost feel sorry for D.J.s, and I have a huge amount of respect for their talents and efforts. The trouble is, so many of them love nothing more than playing back-to-back R & B, and I'm just not an R & B girl. Also, they're far too cool to play 'Saturday Night' or 'Macarena', and they need to know that no one ever had fun because they were trying to be cool. Most D.J.s will tell you they don't really enjoy taking requests and they prefer to work undisturbed. However, if you're smiley, polite and don't mind humiliating yourself ever so slightly by begging for your song repeatedly, they will probably give in to your demands, simply because they know that's the best way to make you go away.

Also, I'll permit some phone use, if you're getting it out in order to share your perfect party playlist. Never leave the house without being D.J.-ready and having a handy hour of crowd-pleasing music to hand, just in case there's an emergency and it falls to you to put on the special big headphones. Try to make friends with D.J.s in your daily life and you can get a bit of a barter system going. You pick up their dry cleaning, they promise you a solid hour of nineties pop bangers.

Exes mean exits

You know what I'm talking about. The music is loud, the beat is jumping through your body, the D.J. is *finally* playing the Vengaboys after you've spent a solid three hours begging them to. You've drained your drink, slid to the floor, flicked your hair and are bent backwards and mid bounce when you see him: the creep who told you he loved you, only to cheat on you on holiday and lie about it to your face, and he still has the audacity to send you the occasional three a.m. WhatsApp.

Do you:

A) Storm over to the bar and demand some throwing ammunition? (And, if you're the sort of person who likes to chuck drinks at people, red wine is the most visually effective, but if you're feeling truly vengeful, get a Baileys – the cream means that, no matter how carefully it's cleaned, their outfit will forever smell slightly of sick.)

B) Pretend you haven't seen him, pull out all of your best moves and dance like you're auditioning for the Pussycat Dolls and you want to make Nicole Scherzinger look like your great-grandmother?

Or, C) Gather your squad and get out of there?

In the short term, option A is enormously satisfying. Throwing drinks over the idiots who have hurt us is a rite of passage during our twenties, up there with learning not to lose our keys every week and working out how to do our laundry without shrinking everything. Everyone gets at least one go – it's a bit like sports day. The trouble is, the boys *love* it. It shows you're hurt enough to care, and they get to think of themselves as some sort of heart-breaking stud, even when they're dripping with Blossom Hill. The best way to hurt them is to properly ignore them, which brings us to option B. I've tried this, and I don't think it's the right answer. It's simply impossible to forget the idiot and have fun when the idiot is metres away from you, and every time you wiggle your bum, you're hoping that he's seeing it and missing it. It's impossible not to look, and there's a chance you might see him flirting with someone else, which doesn't bear thinking about. After spending a lot of time and research on the matter, I've decided that you need to get out of there, pronto. Sadly, this does mean that, if you're out with a friend and her bad ex is looming on the horizon, you need to leave with her – even if the 'Macarena' megamix has just started. There will always be another night out coming up, but friends are precious. If she'd do it for you, you must do it for her.

Get home with the girls

Sometimes, a night presents some exciting romantic opportunities and things get especially flirty. I'm not here to judge anyone, but

101

I will say that, after researching the matter and discussing it with my friends, I've realized that the very best way to end a night out is to leave with the people you arrived with. If you've met someone hot, they'll still be there the next day – and if they're *not*, it's probably not worth hooking up with them after half a pint of Bacardi. Going home in a gang means that you know everyone is safely back in bed, you can remind each other to drink lots of water and you can swap snacks with each other – it's nice to have someone to share a pizza with.

The morning after

Any physicist will tell you that every action has an equal but opposite reaction. At least, I think they will; I vaguely remember something about this from school, but then I also remember trying to make electricity out of a potato, which in retrospect seems completely mad. Anyway, this rule applies to parties: if your action was drinking, dancing, singing your heart out, hugging your friends and telling them how much you love them, the reaction will involve sitting still, drinking water, trying to keep the water down and wondering how you can possibly have motion sickness when you're just sitting still on the sofa. Even though the morning after a big night out has sometimes made me wonder whether it's time to start planning my funeral, they can also be the most fun part of all. Here's why I love them. Plump up your sofa cushions, knock back a Berocca, take a deep breath and join me in hailing the hangover.

Hangovers are hysterical

It doesn't take much to make me laugh, but, on a hangover, everything is funny. This isn't about having a wry chuckle at a picture of a cat trying to make friends with a glove, on the Internet; this is the sort of silliness that involves laughing until you're crying, discovering the remnants of last night's eyeliner have made their way to your ears and then crying some more. I wish I could tell you about my funniest hungover morning, but I can't, because it's impossible to remember what it was that made me laugh so much. I just know I giggled until I ached. Also, if you have smug friends who leap up at seven a.m. to run off their excesses, remember this: a good belly-laugh isn't just more fun, it's probably better exercise.

You're never the worst one

Before we start to see the funny side, it's normal to wake up filled with horror and dread. I know what it's like to lie under your duvet with one eye open, scrolling through your phone, trying to piece together a night, and suddenly have a flashback to singing 'Life Is A Rollercoaster' – although, this might be a level of shame known only to me and Ronan Keating. The worst thing about sobering up after a period of drunkenness is the part where you forget that everyone else was probably just as drunk as you. If you're filled with guilt, don't worry – it's probably OK. Unless you've done something truly heinous, like snogging someone else's boyfriend or stealing someone's taxi, someone will have done something much more embarrassing than you. I have two friends who are too embarrassed to be identified, who were so convinced that they had done something awful the night before that they *called each other*. (And these people do not like talking on the phone.) Barely able to remember anything, they managed to reassure each other that everything was fine and that, if something bad had occurred, the other one would know. Later, they realized they'd ended up at completely different parties and hadn't even seen each other after nine p.m. It's a case of forgive and forget. Forgive yourself, for everyone else has probably forgotten.

Wear your pyjamas to brunch

Some mornings, you're glad to hear the birds singing in the trees, you're happy to run a brush through your hair, and you sing in the shower before skipping off to a smart bar for eggs, Bloody Marys and gossip. However, if you've really gone for it the night before, you have two options: you make your friends come over, or you call a cab and put your coat over your dressing gown. Either way, you eat your brunch in nightwear. And you're not having salmon and prosecco, either – you need Doritos and cold pizza. There is a time and a place for smart restaurants, and you don't want lots of elderly men in blazers making disapproving faces over their Sunday lunch as you get the giggles remembering how you tried and failed to execute the 'worm'. Also, most of the nicer places in Chelsea still get really sniffy when you turn up in your slippers.

Staying In

It's simply not always possible to go out seven nights a week. Maybe you have a horribly unreasonable boss who keeps getting cross about the fact that you always walk in two hours late, holding a bacon sandwich. Maybe the staff at your local have started to make comments about how you're 'part of the furniture' and spend more time there than the manager. Maybe your bank keeps ringing you to tell you you're over your overdraft and you have to stop trying to take out £10 at one o'clock in the morning. Anyway, the universe sometimes sends all sorts of messages that tell a girl she should be in her own bed and sleeping soundly before the local foxes start having noisy sex on the pavement outside. Think of it this way: if you keep charging your phone just a little bit before you use it, the battery life will wear out more quickly every time. Sometimes, you need to turn it off, stop touching it and let it get to a hundred per cent in order to get more use out of it. As humans, we're exactly the same. Here's how I recharge.

Turn your phone off – Insta Stories are the worst

All metaphors aside, I need to *actually turn my phone off* if I'm staying in, or at least log out of Instagram. Why? I'm so frightened of FOMO that, if I see someone having fun on Stories, I'm getting dressed and putting my shoes on faster than a Tasmanian devil, hoping to find the fun. Even if it's just my uncle clinking pint glasses with his beer-loving buddies at the Torquay Rotary Club. Trying not to look is like trying not to read *Game of Thrones* spoilers – if you know it's there, it's just too, too tempting to check it out. I say, 'No phone,' to FOMO, otherwise I'd never get any sleep at all.

Let Richard Curtis be your host

My favourite film in the whole world is *Notting Hill*, because it's not just a gorgeous love story, it's about the absolute, utter joy of having fun, funny friends. *Notting Hill* is a perfect film for a night in, because it makes me feel as though I'm hanging out with my best pals, and I don't even have to make them tea! I can just curl up and enjoy their company. Generally, I don't think you can go wrong with Richard Curtis. I'm always up for making it a double bill with *Four Weddings*. But I think the important thing is to relax with something cosy and comforting that you adore. You don't want to chill out on your own and suddenly find yourself worrying about imaginary zombies.

Feast on fabulously freaky snacks

My favourite pizza topping is a controversial one, but I don't think you can beat a customized Domino's with chicken and tuna. It's not weird, it's a perfect combination of tastes and textures, and I won't talk to anyone who doesn't get it, unless they can tell me, hand on heart, that they've tried it. Go on – I promise you'll be converted. Seriously, I've eaten poisonous insects and liquidized kangaroo bumhole, and yet some people still think chicken and tuna is odd. Anyway, the bliss of a quiet night in is that you can order anything you like on your pizza, and no one needs to know. Even anchovies. I won't tell anyone. You can also do heavenly horrible stuff, like putting your Ben and Jerry's in the microwave, or having peanut butter on garlic bread. It's our seriously revolting secret!

Go to someone else's – and you still feel like you've gone out!

At the moment, I live by myself and I love it, but sometimes I really miss the fun of having flatmates. When you live with people you love, it's much easier to stay in, because a quiet night can get really jolly. Open some wine and you can even have a quick boogie in your PJs before falling into bed! My favourite thing to do on a Sunday is to go and see my best friends, for film watching, snacks and chats. I'm also much less tempted to sneak out if I'm having fun with friends, because I don't need to go out looking for it. Even if it's the middle of the day, I recommend suggesting a sleeping-bag policy – the slumber-party vibe never stops being enjoyable. Also, if you think you might fall asleep and stay over, do bring your toothbrush. If that really is far too much effort, just make everyone come to yours.

How to banish the Sunday blues

OK, so, I need to admit that I might be the only person in the world that I know who doesn't suffer from the Sunday scaries. For me, it all comes back to school. I *loved* school and, because I boarded, I'd always associate Sunday with the excitement of the week ahead. Weekends in Devon with my family were lovely, but *so* long and sleepy. By the time Sunday afternoon arrived, I was desperate to get back to my friends so I could find out all of the gossip.

However, I know loads of people who really struggle to stay sunny on a Sunday. It makes sense. Weekends never seem long enough, do they? We bounce out of bed on Friday, knowing we have just a few more hours to get through before the fun starts. Then, there's forty-eight hours to cram in friends, lovers, laundry,

> 6 Even if it's the middle of the day, I recommend suggesting a sleeping-bag policy – the slumber-party vibe never stops being enjoyable. 9

partying, relaxing, lunches, brunches, dinners and drinks. Weekends make us ambitious. We set ourselves so many goals, and we often struggle to get even halfway through the list.

Sometimes, now, I'll promise myself a quiet weekend, knowing I need to catch up on my sleep and do something about the unwashed mugs piling up in the kitchen sink. Then, suddenly, it will be ten p.m. on Sunday night, and I'm feeling exhausted, having done too much and unable to find a single clean mug to make myself a cup of tea. But staying in isn't the answer either – you just get stuck in a social-media hole, feeling miserable and wondering why everyone else is having a better weekend than you. I do think this is one part of modern life that has made Sundays so much harder for everyone. Before we started posting pictures of all our activities, you felt as though you'd had a successful Sunday if you'd gone dancing and then had a big, delicious lunch. Now, we're all expected to decorate cupcakes, stay up to watch the sunrise and go hiking in the woods. What are you supposed to do if you're having a day of domestic admin? You can hardly Instagram the big Ikea; the lighting is *dreadful*.

This might sound unspeakably dreary, and I apologize for my negativity. I really do adore my weekends. But I promise that, if you struggle with Sundays, you're definitely not alone, and I can help you find a way to make Sunday night feel every bit as exciting as Friday night. Remember, the beginning of the week has the potential to be very exciting indeed. If you dread it, you'll look for the worst and find all sorts of things to worry about, but if you can see the good in a Sunday night, you're setting yourself up for the best week ever. It doesn't matter what sort of week you've had before; you can leave it all behind. You might be about to fall in love, or get promoted, or invent a brand-new cocktail that changes the world. Think of all the Sundays that started with a feeling of doom, which led to Mondays, Tuesdays and Wednesdays where something brilliant happened! And it won't be Sunday night forever. Friday is always right around the corner.

Don't forget that it's still the weekend

I think the biggest mistake that people make about Sundays is to simply brand them Monday Eve and focus on the feelings of doom that they associate with work or school. Sunday is a glorious day in itself, and if you don't make an effort to banish the blues, you're wasting half a precious weekend! That's fifty per cent! My maths is rubbish and even I know that's a serious statistic! Usually, I'm not a big believer in forward planning. I love acting on impulse and making my social life fit with my mood. The best parties aren't scheduled and tightly organized, they just sort of happen. However, if you're not a fan of Sundays, you need to start tackling them with military precision. If you commit to fun, and force yourself to have it, you'll forget to feel sad. Book cheap theatre tickets and get dressed up for the evening. If the play is great, you'll be too distracted to feel gloomy, and if it's awful, you'll be so delighted that it's over that you'll go to sleep in a great mood!

Make your bedroom into a relaxation room

I've spoken about this before, but, for me, my hardest Sunday nights were when I found myself suddenly single. I'd got used to going to bed with my lovely boyfriend and having someone to cuddle as the weekend finished. Then he broke up with me, and the bed felt much too big. I was so aware of the empty space beside me that I might as well have had a duvet cover embroidered with the words *HE CHEATED ON YOU*. Horrid, right? I knew I had to take control and make sure that I could celebrate that space and make my bed a happy place once again, especially on a Sunday night.

It's much more easily said than done, but I like to keep my room as uncluttered as possible, because it helps me to feel calm, and calmness is the one thing you really need to achieve before the week starts up again. Sunday is a great day to change your sheets, because going to bed with freshly laundered linen makes you feel as though everything is new and exciting. It's like being given a brand-new workbook at school, after covering your old one with Tippex lists of all the boys you fancy, just before you go off them.

Also, I love lighting a scented candle, but choose carefully. A little bit of lavender is incredibly relaxing, but some scents are designed to keep you awake and revived. I tried a lemon one once and sleep was impossible – I kept feeling as though someone was going to make me leap out of bed and do some washing up. Also, promise me that you will never, ever go to sleep with a candle burning. I've made some seriously silly mistakes when it comes to housekeeping, but I've never caused a major fire. If you wake up and the room is in flames, you really will have a horrible Monday morning.

Go out – and make an occasion of it

This is a controversial one, but it works. You can destroy those sad Sunday vibes by making Sunday night into the biggest event of the week. Of course, if you do a very complicated, demanding job, this isn't the best idea. If you're a doctor who has to go into surgery at eight o'clock on Monday morning, stay off the Jägerbombs – but you don't have to drink to have a fabulous time. You can go *out* out, or you can leave your house and celebrate Sunday in someone else's. It still counts. Once, I was at my friends' house, and we were all eating pizza in our pyjamas, when I realized that, if we made an effort, slobbing out could feel much more glamorous. A few feather boas and a ballgown later, we were having the time of our lives. The best way to deal with Sunday is to go against nature and make a bit of an effort, while the rest of the world watches the *Antiques Roadshow*.

> ❛ I have to turn my phone off when I stay in as I suffer from severe FOMO. ❜

If being on *Made in Chelsea* has taught me anything, it's that we all have a repressed artist inside us – and you don't have to be Picasso to let it out, you just need to chill a bit. Everyone I know finds that a few crafts can cure the Sunday blues. Some of the boys paint, Olivia likes to get her camera out, and Mark-Francis simply poses while someone else sculpts him in bronze. Doing something crafty can lift your mood and distract you from anything that's making you sad. If you're spending Sunday within a hundred yards of the King's Road, I recommend finding a sushi-making class or a flower-arranging session to put a smile back on your face – you'll definitely run into some trustafarians who are struggling with the back-to-work blues, even though they don't really have proper jobs. Alternatively, you could take a leaf out of Proudlock's book and paint a picture that combines your face with those of your two best buddies. They'll love it! Although they'll probably find it slightly terrifying, too!

Plan something lovely for Monday morning

Ultimately, Sundays themselves aren't bad at all. If we have a bad reaction to them, it's because we're filled with anxiety about the fact that Monday is coming. So, make Monday fun! You could plan a delicious breakfast meeting – you'll feel super-efficient and it is much, much easier to leap out of bed early if you know that you're on your way to waffles. Or book a treat – some people say that a blow-dry is what makes them feel ready to embrace the week ahead, and it makes everyone in their office sit up straight and think that they're a bit of a power player. (Be careful with this one. When you add a crisp shirt and a good night's sleep, you'll look like a superhero. If you wear it with a crumpled dress and smudgy eyeliner, everyone will assume that you're going on a date – or that you're just coming back from one.)

Work Hard, Play Hard

When you're looking for life lessons, you can always find some great advice if you sit down and watch an old-fashioned musical. They taught me everything I know. For example, after seeing *Oliver!* a thousand times, I know that nothing good can come of moving in with a strange, scruffy man you've just met on the street, no matter how friendly he seems – especially if he has an enormous collection of expensive watches. Also, anyone who refuses you a second helping of food is a meanie, and doesn't have your best interests at heart. Watching *Annie* made me realize that a dog is one of the best friends a girl can ever have, that you're not living your best life if, like Miss Hannigan, you end up wearing your dressing gown for more than two days in a row, and that it's important to keep hoping, no matter what. But I think the most educational musical out there might be *Mary Poppins*. Sure, Mary can be terrifyingly strict, she seems to spend most of her time on rooftops and she favours the sort of hats that would get her kicked out of the Royal Enclosure at Ascot. However, she truly believes that work can be fun. In fact, she thinks it *should* be fun, and it's up to us to make it so.

One of the things that I love the most about my life is that I've found a job that I adore. I don't really have to try very hard when it comes to channelling Mary and finding the fun. However, I've done jobs where seeking out the positive has required some serious searching. Still, that doesn't mean I couldn't manage it. In fact, for a few months, I was a real-life Mary Poppins and worked as an actual nanny! Here's my CV. You might be surprised by some of the entries, but hopefully it's proof that we can all find our dream job, no matter how we start out. Some of us are on a career motorway, and cruise straight to our destination without going below seventy miles an hour. And some of us, like me, take a scenic route, getting lost down country lanes, experiencing metaphorical and literal engine trouble, and we spend the journey realizing we wouldn't be having nearly such a nice time if we'd bothered following a map.

2010: *Chief tea-maker and telephone answerer*

When I was twelve, I knew I wanted to become a lawyer. Well, I *thought* I knew that's what I wanted. I've always loved the idea of fighting for justice and protecting people who need help. I adored doing work experience at a local solicitors' office, and although I was too young to do any legal work, I did protect a lot of clever, talented people from hot-beverage dehydration and biscuit short-ages. Also, I discovered a hidden talent for talking on the phone. People hardly ever ring each other up for a chat anymore, and I think the phone call is due a big comeback! Here's a brilliant tip: if you're answering someone else's phone, always say, 'I think they're in a meeting. I'll just check.' This means that the caller will give up and go away if they've just phoned to be annoying about PPI.

2011–12: Loo cleaner and bar worker

These were separate jobs, but they taught me a huge amount about other people. We all have much more in common than we think. It doesn't matter whether you're a busy working mum, a banker, a baker, or a billionaire who has just got off a massive yacht – we all need to use the loo, and you will usually forget to get any cash out and will have to pay for a Diet Coke with a contactless card. Honestly, I think that everyone should have to work as a full-time loo cleaner for at least a week. No one is too grand to snap on a pair of Marigolds and unleash the Toilet Duck. Admittedly, I was so bad at cleaning loos that they had to hire a more experienced person to tackle the toilet, but at least I tried. Working in the pub was much harder, because I kept forgetting where I was, pouring myself a drink after I'd served the customer, and having a chat.

2012–13: Law student

This was the first major part of my career path that did not go to plan. When I started my degree at the University of Westminster,

> ❝ I think that everyone should have to work as a full-time loo cleaner for at least a week. No one is too grand to snap on a pair of Marigolds and unleash the Toilet Duck. ❞

I saw myself as a cross between Elle Woods in *Legally Blonde* and Ally McBeal, with a dash of Judge Rinder. I did not realize that I'd spend most of my time sleeping through alarms and crying in the library. Later, I'll tell you all about what it's like when your lifelong dream turns into a nightmare, but the best thing about dropping out of uni was what it led to, including . . .

2013: Nanny

I truly believe that, if I hadn't gone into T.V., I would still be doing this job. I *loved* nannying. Admittedly, I was not exactly the strictest nanny in the world. I adored my two girls, and hated making them do their homework, so we'd get home from school and put *Harry Potter* on until I knew their parents were approaching. We'd have five minutes to make the house look spick and span, and as soon as they walked through the door, we'd all be studying, looking serious.

At the time, there was one big love in my life – the Toffmobile. It was a ten-year-old Mini Cooper that was less reliable than a builder that comes to your door on a horse, wearing a ten-gallon hat. But I adored it, and I'd bundle the girls into the back and drive them around town in it. I wasn't earning very much money, and I'd try to get as far as I could on as little petrol as possible – basically, trying to get a lot of banger for my buck – which didn't help the Toffmobile's level of reliability. It turns out that £3 of fuel isn't *quite* enough to get you all the way down the Fulham Road. I had to ring the parents and plead for a push.

This job taught me two very important things. Firstly, if you've made a mistake, the best way to fix it is to admit to it and ask for help. Secondly, messing up can be hilarious, and it's much easier to get over something when you're prepared to see the funny side. And watching your ancient car getting towed past shops that sell handbags that cost ten times as much as its scrap value is very funny indeed.

2013: Door person and clipboard monitor

If you want to succeed at anything, the best way to do it is to set yourself a clear, straightforward objective, and then go for your life. Now, I got a job at Embargo because it was one of my favourite places in Chelsea, and my first objective was to combine business with pleasure. I was spending so much time there that I thought I might as well try to get something more significant out of the experience than a hangover. Also, if my local club was also my place of business, I wouldn't have to pay so much to get in, and I might even get a couple of free shots. – at least I'd break even and have a tiny bit of extra petrol money!

I was in charge of ticking off the guest list, and it was my job to sell the V.I.P. tables. I was what they call a motivated seller. As soon as all of the tables were sold, I could put the pen down, dash upstairs and have a boogie – so, whenever I was on the door, every table was gone by eleven p.m. If an elderly man, who had got lost after taking his dog out for a short evening stroll, came to the door to ask for directions, I'd direct him straight to the bar for an ice bucket and a bottle of Stolichnaya. Selling tables meant dancing on them later. I don't think I have many talents or skills, but I *was* absolutely brilliant at this.

2014–present: Professional Chelsea Girl

Let's be real: when your nickname is Toff, you're bound to experience a little bit of nominative determinism in your life. Maybe it was inevitable that I'd end up appearing on a reality show with lots of posh people. Every day, I'm grateful that I got the chance to be in *Made in Chelsea*. It's such fun! I get to spend a lot of time with my friends and I'm always meeting lovely people who watch the show. My favourite moments are when I realize how it unites people. I know families where daughters, mums and grannies all watch it together!

I joined *Made in Chelsea* just after my nineteenth birthday, so, if you're a fan of the show, you've probably seen me grow up. In some ways, it's a bit weird to realize that there are people who know so much about my life, even though I've never met them. However, I love sharing, I've always been really open, and it's not in my nature to hide who I am, so being on reality T.V. suits me perfectly.

Toffolo family album

THEN...

Always smiling even then (despite the hairstyle!) Me aged one.

And here, rocking a fringe and smocking. Okay, so it took me a while to get my hair right! Aged two (taken in the photobooth at Mothercare, just in case you were taken in by the background).

Once a party girl, always a party girl. Aged three, holidaying in Marbella.

Daddy's girl!

Family dinner with my favourite peeps.

I find I always play the cello so much better when
I'm dressed in a tiger suit.

Getting ready to make a splash
Down Under. Me, aged ten, on
Manly Beach, Sydney. Taken
on Boxing Day 2004, the day
of the Tsunami.

I loved being a bridesmaid.
Mum looks great here too!

Demonstrating my mean double-handed backhand.
Aged twelve at Torquay Lawn Tennis Club in the
under-14s tournament.

I might be the smallest girl here, but I got the biggest cup! Here I am, aged eleven, with my mates Emma, Amy and Olivia. I was Head Girl of my school and here I am with the cup to prove it!

NOW . . .

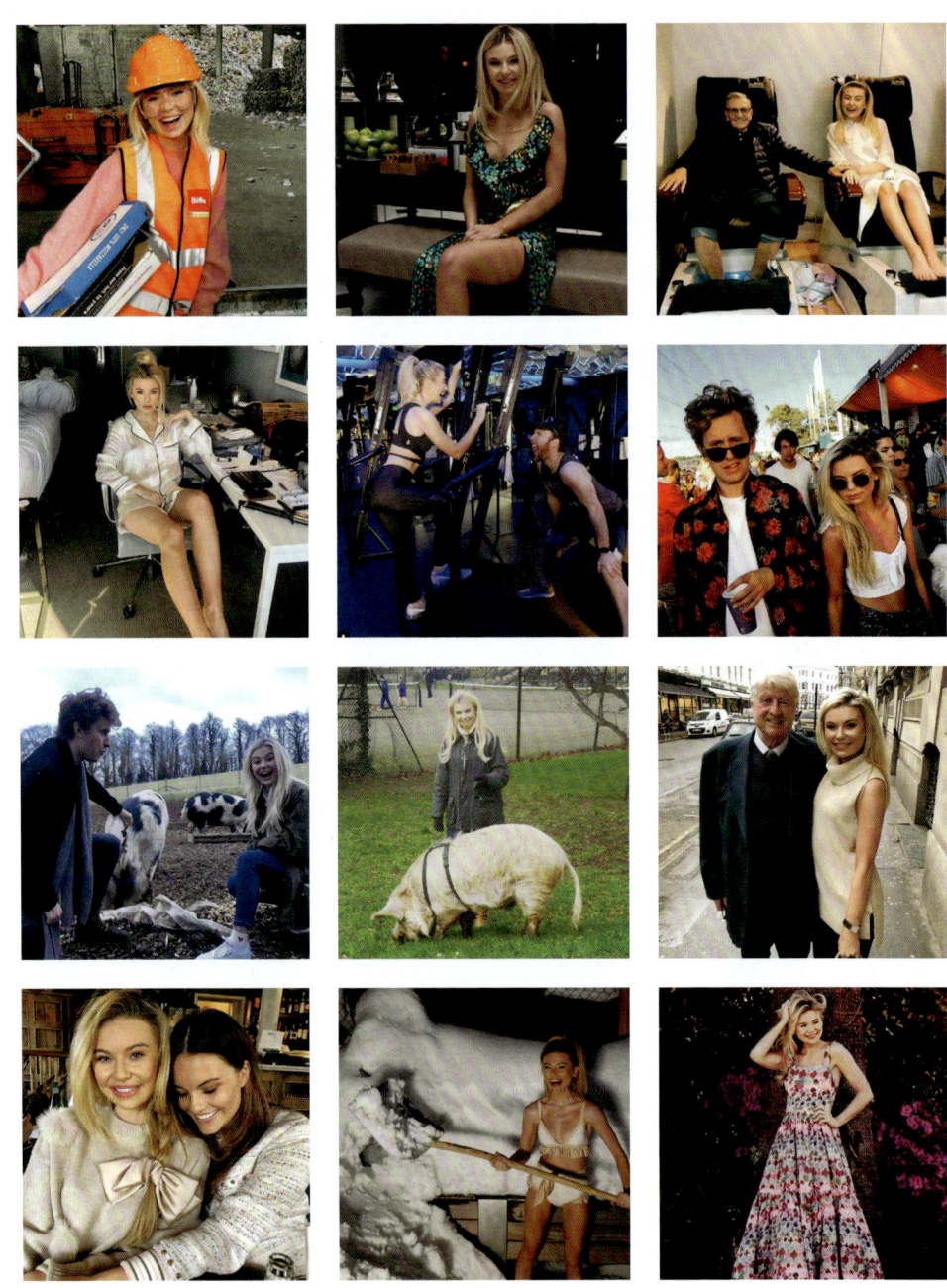

What if I fall?
Oh, but my darling
what if you fly?

2015–present: Editorial assistant, The Lady

Being on *Made in Chelsea* takes up a surprising amount of time – we can spend up to ten days filming for a single hour of telly! But I do have what my parents would call a 'proper' job, too – a job where I have to be at a desk every morning, being productive and looking presentable, no matter what happened the night before. Even if I haven't had enough sleep I've always gone home, showered, changed, brushed my teeth and behaved as though I've had a ten p.m. bedtime and nothing stronger than a peppermint tea.

I love writing, and I've always adored magazines, so working in publishing is a fantastic opportunity for me. Also, I work with some of the cleverest and most fascinating people I've ever met. Some of them have been in the industry for years and have worked on some of the most iconic titles in the world. Every time I go into the office, I learn something new, and this job has taught me that the best way to get the most out of life is to ask as many questions as possible. However, I've also learned that there's a time and a place for this. The best time for a chat is when the issue has just gone to press and all is calm. (The worst is when everyone is running up and down the office, literally *screaming* for coffee.)

2017–present, Jungle Queen

Nothing could have prepared me for what I faced when I flew out to Oz – but then, a bit of me wonders whether every single moment of my career was really some sort of dress rehearsal for jungle life. I've spent my life hoping everything is going to go brilliantly, and laughing off the odd disaster.

Nannying was brilliant practice when it came to bonding with grumpy, hungry campmates. When you get a group of people who are used to life's luxuries, and you dump them in the middle of nowhere, without access to basic plumbing or a toaster, they start behaving like under-tens – and, thanks to that job, dealing with under-tens is my speciality.

At *The Lady*, I've learned to fake it to make it, mainly – to look, speak and act like a lady, even when deadlines are coming at me like speeding cars and I'd quite like to have a sneaky nap under my desk. So, when the pressure – and insects – piled up, I remembered that I knew how to smile my way through any situation.

The best bit about all of the different jobs I've done is that I've met hundreds, maybe thousands of different people. And we all have one big thing in common: literally no one really knows what they're doing. Sure, we all have areas of expertise and bits of our jobs that we're good at, but I'm certain that, every day, every single person has a moment of panic when they realize they're completely clueless and are just guessing their way through. Once you know that, you'll soon realize that you can do anything. If you have a dream job, you don't need to be the cleverest or most qualified person in the room. You just need to be confident enough to have a go, and be prepared to embrace the mistakes you'll make along the way.

How to quit a job

Sometimes, working is a lot like falling in love. And sometimes, you have to take your job by the hands, look deeply into its eyes, take a deep breath and say, 'I'm so sorry. It's not you, it's me.' My dad has been doing the same job since I was little. But I'm in my twenties and I'm part of a generation who change their careers as often as they change their sheets. In fact, some of my stinkier, lazier friends probably change their careers more often than their duvet covers.

No one expects you to have the same job forever, which means there's no reason to stay in a job that's making you horribly unhappy. We'll all do work we don't always love, but we must avoid the jobs that make us feel sad and crush our confidence. I quit my degree because it was crushing me. Usually, I laugh my way through life, and I pride myself on being able to find the positive side to any situation. When I started studying, I was stuck. I adore reading, and I was so excited about growing, learning and getting ready to embark upon a serious career. It was such a shock to discover that I'd made a mistake. Not the kind that meant putting my hand up and asking a silly question in a lecture – that's the sort I don't mind making. This was about my future, and I had to ask myself some serious questions about who I was and what I wanted. The situation was so stressful that I started to struggle with my skin. I'd never had any problems with my complexion, but I started to break out. I felt sad and self-conscious. It was as if the universe was telling me to step back and make some serious decisions.

Usually, we tell people that, if something's hard, it means it's worth doing. If you're struggling, you'll get a reward. This might be true when you're eight years old and the thing you're struggling with is bedtime or a bowl of broccoli, but the best thing about growing up is getting to know yourself and realizing that, if something doesn't feel right, it's usually better to stop and try something else, rather than squeezing yourself to fit into a space that doesn't suit you. If I'd stayed at uni, I might have made myself miserable for years, and I'd now be doing a job I hated, with a degree I didn't really want. Instead, I have a career that allows me to try something new every single day, and a job that, instead of suppressing my personality, allows me to celebrate it.

I think most careers are the result of a lot of trial and error. We don't have to love everything we do, we just need to be prepared to try lots of different things, and to trust our instincts. The loveliest thing about living in Chelsea is that everyone I know seems to have twenty different careers, and some people's greatest talent is to make the act of being fabulous look like a full-time job. Some of the most successful people I know are serial quitters, and I know really successful, proper grown-ups who wouldn't hire someone unless they've been fired at least once. Ultimately, you can't ever fail if you're doing something that you're truly passionate about.

I thought law was going to be my big passion, but leaving it led me to the work I love, and now I'm happier than ever. I had to fail hard in order to find success. While there's so much about my job that I'm really proud of, I don't define success by having social-media followers, meeting celebrities or even winning my jungle crown. It's about being able to wake up every morning and know that I'm excited about what the day holds, and that I'm doing work that makes me deeply happy. That's the best career advice I can give anyone. Choose to do the thing that makes you feel happiest, and you'll never want to quit.

How to wow in a job interview

Personally, I believe that the worst advice that has ever been given, since the history of advice began, is this: 'Just relax and be yourself.' It's the advice people will give you if you're going to a job interview, and it doesn't help at all. Firstly, 'relax'. You're going into a strange environment, where you'll have to persuade someone you've never met that you're talented, skilled and likeable enough to hang around their office for several hours a day. The pressure is *on*, and you're bound to feel nervous. No one's nerves

' You don't need to be the cleverest or most qualified person in the room. You just need to be confident enough to have a go, and be prepared to embrace the mistakes you'll make along the way. '

129

have ever been cured because someone told them to relax – as if that thought had never occurred to them! Admittedly, 'be yourself' is slightly more useful. We should always be ourselves. There's no point turning up in a suit and saying you'd make a brilliant accountant because you're very good at maths, when working out a tip brings you out in a cold sweat and you only ever used the compass in your geometry set to attempt a bad, home-made tattoo. But which version of yourself should you be? Most of us need to do a bit of an edit – there's the 'me' that can sit at a desk and be sensible, and there's the 'me' that can construct a sentence that only contains the words 'shots' and 'NOW!'

I think the best way to deal with job interviews is to treat them like first dates. On a first date, you're testing for chemistry. Hopefully, you turn up thinking, *Let's see if we like each other, stay chilled and, if it feels right, we'll go from there.* You don't arrive sweaty and terrified, muttering, 'I have to make them like me. It doesn't matter how many lies I tell or how weird and anxious I make them feel, I MUST IMPRESS THEM!' A job interview is a two-sided process, and it gives you a chance to get to know your potential new boss. The biggest mistake that people make is that they're so keen to 'win' the job, they don't stop to think about whether they actually want to do it. When I went for my interview at *The Lady*, I got over my nerves quite quickly because everyone there made me feel so comfortable. As soon as I stepped into the office, I could see myself working there, and that calmed my nerves and helped me to focus.

However, I did have a disaster to deal with. I'd spent ages

selecting the perfect interview outfit. I did plenty of research and knew I needed something formal but feminine, and that I needed something smart enough to impress the grandest duke, while being relatively practical, sensible and not too distracting. It was a situation I rarely find myself in, where neither trainers nor a ballgown would do. So, I found a fabulous tweed jacket. It was pretty, but tailored enough to make me feel quite grown-up. It looked just right for a day in London, but also implied that I'd know what to do if I ever found myself sitting on top of a horse. Ultimately, it was absolutely on brand: a ladylike jacket for *The Lady*, a dreamy statement piece for my dream job. And what happened? I ripped it! Just before I was about to meet the editor and try to land a job I longed for, I discovered a huge tear in the sleeve. Talk about a confidence crisis! You can't go for a job interview at *The Lady* while looking and feeling like a tramp.

Luckily, my friend Jess came to help. Admittedly, our styles are quite different, and what looks incredibly cool on her is not necessarily suitable for a job interview with one of the oldest and most respected magazines in the country. It was very kind of her to offer me her distressed denim, but I think that would have seriously distressed the editor. Still, the important thing was that she came along to support me, and that gave me the boost I needed. She reminded me that it really didn't matter what I wore – clothes could give me confidence, but my new boss was much more interested in my brain and personality than whether or not all of my clothes were intact. I think job interviews can make us all wobble and doubt ourselves. They really test our confidence and make us question everything. Our friends are there to make us feel confident, and they remind us who we are and what we're good at.

In a way, I'm really glad that I had a pre-interview jacket panic. It forced me to address my fears and to work out a method of styling them out. Ultimately, nothing ever goes to plan and you can't prepare for every disaster. You just have to smile and keep going. Also, there's something quite relaxing about a good dilemma. The worst has happened, so you stop worrying about all of the other bad things that *might* happen, and simply get on with it.

Getting your friends to help you prepare for an interview makes the whole process much more fun. Also, you can learn things you never knew about each other by asking some seriously weird questions. Sometimes, interviewers love to put you on the spot, and your actual answer isn't important, but they want to know how you arrive at it. In the USA, Whole Foods asks new staff, 'Would you rather fight one horse-sized duck, or one hundred duck-sized horses?' This is a scary interview question, but it's a debate that will keep you and your friends occupied for an entire evening. For the record, I think I'd definitely pick the second option. Duck-sized horses sound adorable. I'm sure you could work out a way of befriending them, instead of fighting with them. If the worst came to the worst, you could probably just jump over them.

Love

I hope my exes aren't reading this right now, because they might not like the fact that I am about to tell you: I'm not sure that I've ever been in love. Of course, there are plenty of people in my life that I have loved, and still adore, deeply. But, as much as I've liked my boyfriends, none of them has come close to replacing my friends. I've never met anyone that I wanted to stay in with, when I could have been out having fun with my favourite people.

Let me give you an example. Take Valentine's Day, 2016. I hadn't been seeing my boyfriend for long, but he was keen to have a romantic night in. You know – flowers, champagne, lighting the Diptyque candles you've had since Christmas but haven't been able to bring yourself to open because you never feel quite fancy enough. Did I want to spend a chilly February night staying cosy and warm, enjoying fine wine and cuddles? As if! I made my excuses with the boy and spent the night with my best friends, enjoying our traditional Valentine's Day at a cheesy, cheery Italian restaurant on the Fulham Road, with a bring-your-own-bottle drinks policy. Ollie Locke was the ringleader. He's fond of Salcombe gin, and we're convinced there's something in it that sends the sanest, smartest person a bit doolally. So, after a few gins, I was dancing on Ollie's kitchen table and having a sneaky smooch with my friend Richard. Cupid would not have approved.

While that might not have been my finest hour, exactly, it made me realize that there are many kinds of love, and the romantic sort isn't necessarily the best. More importantly, it made me think about where my priorities lie. Having a boyfriend you adore is brilliant, but there's no point wasting time with someone who is almost right; you have to be a perfect fit for each other. My good friend Mark-Francis says it's always better to be alone than badly accompanied. If you're in a relationship with someone who doesn't fill you with joy and make you feel like the best and brightest version of yourself, they're not for you. Personally, I need someone who understands I'd rather go out dancing on the most romantic night of the year than stay in for the sake of tradition.

Love seems like a serious business, but meeting people really should be about having fun. I love a good flirt. You don't need to be outrageously sexy, or withdrawn and mysterious. Flirting is all about showing that you're having fun, and that you're happy in yourself. To be honest, I'm quite casual about it.

Occasionally, I'll complain that I don't meet that many new people, and then a wise friend will say, 'Well, Georgia, if you spent a bit more time talking to chaps at the bar, and a bit less time jumping up and down on the dance floor, you might have more luck.' Also, I get pied off all the time. (For the uninitiated, this means being humiliated by a potential new crush, who has rejected you – because it's as embarrassing as having a cream pie thrown in your face by a clown. I tell my girlfriends that anyone who rejects them *is* a clown, so they needn't worry.) Still, there's a famous expression about omelettes and eggs, and, in this instance, I think it translates to, 'You don't have a hope of finding romantic happiness unless you're prepared to make an idiot of yourself every so often.'

Why being single is brilliant

Firstly, if you're reading this chapter and making notes, I'm *guessing* that you're single and you're hoping to find some tips on dating and meeting people. I promise there will be plenty of those, but at the time of writing, I am properly single for the first time in my adult life. As unattached as a slightly bendy, salty crisp, as they say. It is wonderful. At the moment, I'm standing alone, surveying my landscape and looking forward to the rest of my twenties. It feels as though I'm at the start of an exciting path – I've walked a little way down, but I can still see my front door!

Ever since my teens, there have been a few boys in my life, and while I wasn't properly involved with them, I had someone to message when something exciting happened, and someone who would take me out for a drink and cheer me up when I was feeling low. You make these pacts, and promise each other that you'll give it a go and get married when you're thirty, or forty. I had emergency engagements with half the men in my phone. It's really comforting to have these lovely, easy, flirty friendships, but it's slightly distracting, too.

It's difficult to make space in your head for anything useful, when a bit of you is wondering whether someone likes you, and whether you actually like them. Also, flirting when you're bored is *dangerous*. If you need a quick boost, you can always conjure up a dinner date or an exciting message exchange, when you don't necessarily feel strongly about the person you're contacting. You just think it would be jolly to have a little bit of excitement or attention, because it's much more fun than worrying about the fact that you have no clean laundry, or your boss has just come back from a two-week holiday and you're about to get in trouble because you've done no work for a fortnight. It's a little bit like a drug. Of course, it's perfectly normal and natural to enjoy a bit of attention, but when we start needing it to feel normal, we're in trouble – it can be as addictive as Internet shopping, or Deliveroo. I should know – I've been so addicted to Deliveroo that I had to call them up and get them to disable my account. They once sent me a Nando's delivery in eight minutes – which is quicker than most boys respond to a dinner invite. It's disturbing.

Anyway, whether it's cooking your own meals, or going out to your favourite restaurant and requesting a table for one, I am all for independence. Being single is a great opportunity to get to know yourself. You don't need to make the tiny, constant compromises that come up when you're in a relationship. I think women, especially, can really benefit from putting themselves first. We need to learn what we want and what feels comfortable. If you're newly single and miserable, try to fall in love with yourself first, before you start dating! Most importantly, the people that you draw into your life will be attracted by the vibe you give off. If you feel lonely and desperate for love, the worst boys in the world are the ones who will ask for your number. If you feel as though you love spending time with yourself, you'll find people who love spending time with you, too, for all the right reasons – and they'll be secure enough in themselves to make a relationship work. There is a reason why Beyoncé sings songs about being single, independent and proud, and what's good enough for Beyoncé is certainly good enough for the rest of us!

> 'Be a rum negroni, or a champagne cocktail! A lot of people won't like you, but those that do will adore your complexity, weirdness or effervescence.'

How I got over heartbreak

Although I've been lucky enough to date some of the most dashing men in south-west London, I've only had one very serious

139

relationship. This was with my ex-boyfriend, James, who broke my heart into a million pieces when I heard from my friends that he was seeing someone he worked with behind my back. I didn't know exactly what to believe, but this really undermined our relationship because obviously all the trust was gone. Now, if any of my friends are ever cheated on, I rush to their side and tell them that it's not their fault at all. If you've ever been in this situation, you need to know that *no one* makes their boyfriend or girlfriend cheat. It never, ever happens because you're not good enough for them. In fact, it's the opposite. Anyone who cheats on you is not good enough for you. They don't cheat because they think someone else is prettier, or funnier, or more talented. Sometimes, it's because they feel insecure in themselves, or they're worried about the relationship and their head is in a strange place. When someone cheats on you, *they* have made a mistake. Not you.

However, as someone who has been in this horrible situation, I know that all the logic in the world can't numb the pain of heart-break, and you do have moments when you worry that you might actually die. You feel like a girl in an old novel – perhaps Jane Eyre, or one of those Austen heroines that catches pneumonia just because she went out for an unusually long walk. Being cheated on makes you feel horribly anxious and insecure. Everything in your world stops making sense, and you divide your life into periods of BC and AD – Before Cheating and After the Dickhead ruined everything. Love songs make you cry. The Vengaboys make you cry. You plot your nights out obsessively, because you're deter-mined to show the person that hurt you that you don't miss them at all, even though you spend all of your money on dresses because you're convinced that, if you bump into them looking hot enough, they'll beg to have you back.

James told me that he wanted to break up, and it came out of the blue. He arrived at my flat, the place where we'd spent a million minutes together – eating meals, drinking wine, kissing, giggling and creating happy memories – and he told me that he didn't want to be with me anymore. The news came out of nowhere. I felt as though I'd pressed a button to call a lift, and then walked through the open doors to discover the lift had disappeared and I was plummeting towards the ground so fast that I'd left my heart on the top floor. I felt weak and wobbly, but I was determined to carry on. When I went out, I bumped into a friend. 'Have you seen James? He's with his new girlfriend!' grinned the friend, who didn't realize that everything still felt so raw. I thought I was going to be sick.

I'm telling you this because I need you to know that heartbreak happens to everyone. It's perfectly OK to feel as though it's the end of the world, and that you'll never get over it. You'll feel desperately sad and insecure, and question every single thing about yourself. And you *will* get better, I promise. When you're going through the most horrible feeling in the world, you'll feel overwhelmingly weak, but you'll come out of the other side feeling so much stronger. You'll be unbeatable. Also, I suspect that, from the outside, my life looks pretty much perfect. I have lovely friends, a lovely job and a *very* covetable pair of Chanel pumps. None of those things protected me from the horror of heartbreak.

It's only now I realize that I was the only person who felt as though I was a giant loser at the time. From the outside, it looked like I was doing OK. My friends worried about me and wanted to make it better, but no one was laughing at me. So, I promise that, if you've been hurt in love and you feel as though you're falling apart, no one is laughing at you, either. It doesn't matter how desperate and miserable you feel, most of the world thinks you've got it together. Also, think about all of the famous people who have been cheated on. Beautiful film stars with Malibu mansions and cupboards full of Oscars have probably experienced the same feelings as us. Experiencing heartbreak doesn't make you less of a person, but working through it might be the making of you.

Eventually, after a few months, James told me that he'd made a mistake and wanted me back. Perhaps I should have laughed in his face and said, 'Ha! Yes, you made a big mistake! Huge!' and blocked his number. But I'm only human, and we started dating again. Now, some people might not think that was my smartest move, but I still had feelings for him. They say that ghosts haunt us because they have unfinished business on Earth. At the time, I was so spooked by my experience that it felt as though my love life was being conducted by Patrick Swayze and Demi Moore. I needed to lay some spirits to rest – and, to coin a cliché, I'd say that I needed closure.

Trying again with James made me realize that a good relationship is built on trust, and I couldn't trust him anymore. Rationally, I believe that he made a silly mistake, and probably wouldn't do it again, but deep down I felt as though something had changed, and I just couldn't be sure of him. I'm glad we gave it another go, because I learned so much about myself. I worked out where my boundaries lie and why I can't be with someone who crosses them. We decided to call it off when I went into the jungle, and it was partly because I knew that I'd be worrying about him while I was away. I was going into a situation where I had no phone, no idea of what was going on in the outside world, and I didn't want to miss out on the fact that I was in one of the most beautiful and exotic locations I'd ever visited because I was obsessed with who James might be with in the 151 Club.

Breaking up with him is definitely the most grown-up decision I've ever made, and it makes me feel incredibly proud of myself. We're still friends – and practically neighbours – but I was able to end the relationship on my own terms, which feels really healthy. When we briefly got back together, I realized that no relationship is ever simple or straightforward. I saw everything in black and white after he cheated on me, when there were so many shades of grey (which is ironic, since having my heart broken is the most unsexy thing I've ever experienced. It's about as erotic as taking your bins out.) Since our break-up, I've been able to invest so much energy into my career. I admit that it's very satisfying to realize that he knows everything is going well for me at work, and that being single suits me. The best revenge is living well. I think the seventeenth-century poet, George Herbert, said that, but, then again, it might have been Mark-Francis.

I used to think that going to sleep by myself on a Sunday night seemed so miserable, and I'd miss having someone to cuddle.

Now, I spread out like a starfish and I adore the fact that I have my own space, both in my bed and in my brain. Your bed and your heart are incredibly special, sacred spaces, and you should be extremely fussy about who you let inside.

Dealing with a dumping

Firstly, remember that IT IS NOT YOUR FAULT. Make up a chant, set a reminder on your phone, write this on your arm in Sharpie if you have to. But do your best not to worry or obsess that you might still be together, if you'd done things differently. *They* did this, and the time will come when you feel as though you've had a lucky escape, I *promise*. Don't beat yourself up.

Follow your feelings. You're in shock. The break-up might have come out of the blue, and, if that's the case, you'll feel quite traumatized. Try to focus on doing what feels right, rather than what you think you ought to do. It's OK to cry. It's fine to stay in. You might want to go out. Other people will give you plenty of advice about what you should be doing, and you can ignore them if you want. This is your break-up.

Organize a cleaning rota. Don't worry, you don't have to do any cleaning! You won't feel like looking

> As someone who has had their heart broken, I know that all the logic in the world can't numb the pain of a break-up.

after yourself, but you'll need clean hair and clean pyjamas. Your best friends will want to help you, so ask if they can give you a hand with things like washing up and laundry. Everything will feel slightly less awful if you have clean bedsheets, especially if you're staying in a lot.

Prepare for your mood swings to go public. You will feel like a furious, hormonal thirteen-year-old all over again. I've said, 'I'm fine, I'm definitely over him,' then burst into tears, *then* thrown a cushion at the wall, all in the same hour. You won't feel one hundred per cent better straight away, but every moment that finds you feeling a bit better is proof that you're on the mend.

Know that this won't last forever. Your feelings will be so sad, complex and intense that you won't feel as though you can ever recover, and then, one day, something will mysteriously click into place and you'll feel as though you've just returned from an out-of-body experience. I was in hell for two weeks and suddenly I felt fine. It's a little bit like having appendicitis. At the time, it doesn't seem as though the pain will ever end, but the next day you're up and about, and ready for a burger.

Dealing with rejection

One good thing about being horribly broken-up with and broken-hearted is that you laugh in the face of rejection. It seems silly. You've been to hell and back, and once you've survived that, there is nothing you can't do. You can't be bothered to care if someone doesn't want to have dinner with you – and this is great news, because London is literally littered with men who don't want to have dinner with me!

You can't meet someone amazing unless you're prepared to put up with some rejection first, any more than you can buy a brilliant dress on the Internet without sending back at least three dresses that make you look as though you're smuggling a Swiss roll in your bra. It's the law of averages. As the philosophers of Instagram are quick to tell us, you miss a hundred per cent of the shots you don't take. Or rather, wear your heart on your sleeve, pursue the people who make you feel passionate and, if it doesn't work out, have some shots!

I think that, for most of us, our greatest fear is that we're going to be humiliated, and everyone will know and laugh at us. One way to confront that fear is to stare it in the face and say, 'Bring it on!' This is why I quite like asking people out on social media, where everyone can see. It's much easier to laugh it off, if it happens in public, and you can pretend you weren't being serious. It feels a bit more significant when you're rejected over DM. Not everyone is going to adore you, or understand you, and you have to work through the numbers in order to get to the people who do.

The way I see it, we're all, ultimately, like cocktails. You could be a vodka, lime and soda. Reasonably popular, totally inoffensive, and nobody's favourite. Everyone will want to hang out with you on a night out, but no one will remember you. When people speak about the best drinks they ever had, no one ever says, 'Oh my God, I was in this really sketchy bar in Paris, which was practically deserted, and the bartender mixed the best vodka soda I've ever had! It tasted so plain and safe!' Be a rum negroni, or a champagne cocktail! A lot of people won't like you, but those that do will *adore* your complexity, weirdness or effervescence. Yes, people can be fizzy, too!

So, when someone turns you down, it doesn't mean that you're not gorgeous, funny and fabulous. It simply means that they're looking for an icy Chablis or a dirty Martini, and your flavours aren't for them. With practice, you'll learn not to take it personally, and you'll realize that they've done you a favour because they probably weren't right for you, either.

When you open yourself up to being rejected, dating feels less risky because you've opened yourself up to the worst thing that can happen, and you're embracing it. Also, you have the chance to learn about letting people down gently, which is an extremely valuable skill. I'm a firm believer in going out and getting to know people whenever you have the chance. After all, there are fourteen lunch and dinner slots in any given week, and you might as well spend some of them discovering different people to flirt with. Most of us can usually tell within five minutes whether or not a date will be a dud. However, I believe that anyone can be interesting and entertaining if you ask the right questions. You're not signing up for a lifetime together, just lunch. Also, don't forget that you might not be sitting opposite the love of your life, but, for all you know, they're the neighbour, brother or best friend of your next grand romance. Pretend you're a journalist and you're writing a profile for a newspaper. It's up to you to find something exciting about them – you just need to get good at probing. This is the best way to make friends. Remember, if a stranger is a friend you haven't met, a bad date is simply a friend you decided not to snog.

Being friends with your exes

Almost everyone I date ends up being a good friend. This is because I am practically a modern-day saint, and instead of attracting woodland animals with my gentle nature, I attract former flings who want to bask in my holy presence. OK, that's not entirely true. The real reason is because everyone I date lives no more than about three streets from me, and if we weren't friends with each other, then every trip to Waitrose would be fraught with anxiety and despair. Honestly, being friends with your exes does not come easily, and I've really worked hard to master the skill. It's definitely one of the most grown-up things I've ever done, up there with hand-washing my bras and remembering to turn all of the lights off before I go on holiday.

My friend Richard is someone that I had a bit of a fling with, and getting over him was hard. He's a little bit older than me and, at the time, he was the one who was mature enough to know that it wasn't working, and he called it off. We weren't serious, but I sulked – being rejected by someone I respected so much really stung. Richard is one of the cleverest people I know: a scientific genius who has actually built robots. When a super-intelligent person says that dating you was not their smartest decision, it hurts harder than stubbing all ten toes on a table leg.

Part of the trouble was that Richard and I shared a group of best friends, and that made life more complicated. I could flounce away, declare myself humiliated and heartbroken, and cut myself off from the people I adored most in the world. Or I could laugh it off, get over myself and grow up. Our friends didn't want to see me miserably obsessing over Richard. It would make things enormously awkward for us all. The sooner I could start smiling my way through it, the sooner our gang would be back to normal. This meant that, instead of focusing on my disappointment, I had to invest my energy into building our friendship back up. The writer Nora Ephron once said, 'Never marry someone you wouldn't want to be divorced from,' and this makes so much sense to me. My version would be, 'Never date, if you couldn't be mates!'

Of course, you can't be friends straight away. If you've been really close to someone romantically, you need to give yourself some time to make the transition back into friendship. Your other friends will understand that you're going to need a few weeks apart, at least. You need to create a brand-new context for your ex. If I can, I like to use this time to see friends and family who live outside of London. The best way to get a little emotional distance and perspective is to put some actual miles between you both.

The hardest part about staying friends with an ex is that they will eventually meet someone else, and you will have to be pleased for them and completely cool about the fact that their new girlfriend wants to come out for dinner with the group. You cannot fantasize about lacing her soup with laxatives, and you certainly can't ask your taxi driver to speed up if you see her on the pavement beside a muddy puddle. If you think that you'll struggle to maintain a positive relationship under these circumstances, it's OK to keep your distance for a bit. You can't force a friendship. However, do remember that time is the most effective remedy of all. It's better than Berocca. The first time you meet your ex's new partner will be difficult and distressing, and then, after a couple of months, you'll have fallen in love and you'll be totally distracted. (Hopefully, your ex will be gratifyingly grumpy about this!)

Ways of making your move

Women, listen to me! This is very important. What year is it? Are we going out by ourselves, earning our own money, paying our rent and choosing our own clothes? Yes! Are we going to balls, dancing quadrilles, wearing surprisingly low-cut floor-length dresses with elbow-length gloves, not speaking until we're spoken to and hoping that some grumpy man will pay attention to us, because everyone thinks he's incredibly important, an idea they're basing on the fact that he has a big house in Hertfordshire? NO! So, why are we still waiting to be asked out? This is our time! We need to be bold, confident and courageous. If we wait for the person we like to make the first move, we're going to be spending a lot of time at home, getting those passive-aggressive Netflix messages asking us why we've been watching *Friends* for three hours.

Looking for your dream date?
Get off the Internet!

Call me old-fashioned, but I am totally over Internet dating. I've tried the apps, and met some nice people, but it's never not awkward when someone spots you and takes a screenshot of your Tinder profile. Also, the loveliest thing about living in Chelsea is that your life is like Tinder. There are hot men everywhere, and instead of looking at your phone, you can look up and watch what's going on from the comfort of the number 22. Try to stop yourself from swiping, though; the bus drivers get quite cross when your fingers smear the windows.

I think it's hard to be relaxed when we're constantly checking our phones, and you need to be relaxed to date properly. When you immerse yourself in real life, you're in a state of flow, and that's a much better position to be in when you're hoping to meet someone. They'll see you at your best and most natural, and you'll have a much clearer idea of whether there's any chemistry between you.

Asking people out is scary, but, over the years, I've got quite good at it. This isn't because I'm one of those skilled, super-confident seductresses who leaves a trail of palpitating men in her wake every time she sprays her perfume. It's because loads of my very best friends are boys, so I know exactly how boys work. The secret is that there really isn't one. Ultimately, boys and girls are basically the same. We all worry about dating, we obsess over the fact that someone hasn't replied for eight hours, even though we can *see* that they've read our WhatsApp, and we all love to be asked out! When you suggest a date to someone, they will be so excited to hear from you that, even if they're not sure about whether you're the one for them, you'll have made their day. It's a huge compliment. I firmly believe that the more compliments you give, the more you get – it's a bit like those loyalty cards that earn you free coffee. (Or you could ask out your hottest local barista, and then you'll definitely get free coffee.)

The most important thing to do is smile. If you see someone you like the look of, don't waste time hoping they notice you. Catch their eye, look cheerful and introduce yourself. Be as natural and friendly as you can. Do *not* use a chat-up line. I can't stress this enough. They are cheesier than the fondue menu of a Swiss ski lodge, and it doesn't matter how funny or ironic you think you're being, you're not going to impress anyone with what is basically a forty-year-old joke. Don't be afraid to give compliments. Some people think that the best way to get someone's attention is to make a slightly mean comment that confuses them. When you've got to know your crush a little better, it's fine to tease and be silly, but when you're introducing yourself, don't make fun of their hair or shoes. They will leave and find a different girl to talk to. Probably someone who likes their shoes. Just think about how you'd like someone to approach you and do the same thing. 'Hello, my name's Georgia. It's lovely to meet you! May I buy you a drink?' These are the words that have never steered me wrong. It works beyond the bar, too – remember, the drink does not have to be alcoholic.

Socially acceptable ways to stalk your ex: the dos and don'ts

I'm not exactly proud of this, but I think it pays to be honest. I've never had an ex that I didn't follow after we broke up. Not follow in a creepy way; it's not the sort of stalking that Sting sings about. If you're even thinking about going through someone's bins, I beg you to stop and have a bath before things get out of hand. I'm talking about low-level stalking – the sort where you're simply choosing to consume all of the information that your ex wants to share. You can tell what they're eating once they've Instagrammed their breakfast; you don't need to check their rubbish for eggshells. Break-ups are hard and, even if a relationship is over, I think that it's important to know what your ex is up to. Because, if they're sharing lots of inspirational quotes about using Buddhism to deal with their pain, you're home and dry. But if they're posting pictures of themselves drinking champagne on yachts, and hot girls keep appearing in their comments, you might have to take action. Here's how it's done.

Do invent a fake Instagram account

I mean, come on. We've all done it. It's the very best way to keep tabs on any old flames, especially if you've unfollowed them immediately after the break-up, in an approximation of dignity that, now you look back on it, was an obvious huff. Invent a secret identity and you can look to your heart's content, and no one needs to know. This is especially handy when your ex goes on holiday with his new girlfriend and you need to say bitchy things about her taste in bikinis. Also, remember there's safety in numbers. Get your friends to join in, and use your fake Insta to stalk everyone's exes! Share the wealth!

Don't make your fake account too interesting

So, for a while, my friends and I were pretending to be Tracy McGinty, vicar's wife and 'Great aunt to three wonderful cherubs.' Of course, none of the exes could think of any logical reason for a vicar's wife to be following them. They didn't even watch *The Vicar of Dibley*. So, to our dismay, one of them worked it out and blocked Tracy. We spent hours in our WhatsApp group trying to figure out what might have tipped them off, but I think that Tracy was slightly too enticing. Next time, we'll pretend to be a really boring insurance company, and share pictures of fax machines with captions talking about a hard day at the office.

Also, don't write about your secret stalking Instagram account in a national newspaper column

I outed Tracy in *The Sunday Times* and now every one of my exes is *extremely* suspicious of me. When there are lots of you sharing the same account, there is also a high risk that one of you will accidentally comment on someone else's pictures when you're logged into the fake account, and then it's game over for all of you.

Do remember they're watching you, too

Once, when I knew that my ex was still logged into my Twitter account on his phone, I made my friend send me DMs, like this one: *Who was that hot guy who was really into you at the party?* Then I got her to follow it up with, *There are so many guys who are into you at the moment, what is going on? You're on fire!* Your ex is probably just as interested in your social media as you are in theirs. Use it to your advantage!

Do 'bump into' them

If you know your ex is in the area, it's completely normal to leave the house in the afternoon in full make-up, high heels and hot-roller hair, for a casual stroll around the neighbourhood. It's also normal to pop into their local for one, and stay until closing time, just in case they turn up.

But don't worry if you actually bump into them and you're not looking your best

The rule of the universe is that you can spend a week wearing all of your best dresses, and more make-up than was used in the last season of *RuPaul's Drag Race*, and your ex will be nowhere to be seen. Yet, they'll emerge when you're hungover in the corner shop with wet hair and no mascara, buying a bumper pack of loo roll. The worst thing you can do is hide. It's incredibly tempting, but it will just make everything more strained and awkward in the long run. Style it out, even though you will feel like you're dying, to the point that you might as well have R.I.P. written on your forehead. Smile, make a joke, offer them a spare loo roll. You probably look a hundred times better than you think you do, and this is someone who is likely to have seen you in worse states. Also, looking scruffy will suggest that you've moved on and you're playing it cool, even if this isn't true at all.

And don't give up hope!

The Internet can be a blessing and a curse, but if you truly believe that you and your ex have a little bit more mileage in the tank, a mix of virtual and real-life stalking might relight their fire and keep you linked to each other for long enough for you to both consider giving it another try. I think I kept my ex interested by using social media to suggest I was busy, popular and happy, even though I missed him like mad. The fact that I seemed to be getting on so well without him definitely forced him to think about me more. If I hadn't used social media, I suspect he might have forgotten me. Of course, this is a high-risk strategy, and it can make you miserable. If you genuinely want to get over someone and move on, it might be best to stay off social media altogether.

Confidence

Sometimes, I suspect that south-west London might be the confidence capital of the world. If you get off the Tube at Sloane Square, you'll notice that almost everyone you see is walking around as though they own half of Knightsbridge and they decided not to buy the other half because there weren't enough champagne bars for them. They loll about Hyde Park as though it were their own back garden and swing their shopping bags with the self-assurance of a *Strictly* pro, whether they've just come out of Moncler or Marks and Spencer. Even the dogs strut around smartly, as though there's Pol Roger in their Pedigree.

Admittedly, this can tip into overconfidence – or, rather, arrogance – which is something we all want to avoid. There is such a concentration of confidence that it would be nice to see it shared all over the country – although, when I'm seeing my family in

Devon, I see plenty of different examples. In Chelsea, the vibe could be summed up as, 'Get out of my way, for I am extremely busy and important!' In Torquay, the spirit is a bit more, 'I'm not getting out of anyone's way; I am going to enjoy taking my time; I don't care if you're late to meet the Queen or rushing to the hospital for a brain-transplant operation.' Honestly, I love both approaches, although I might feel less positive about the last one next time I'm sitting in traffic in the town centre.

Anyway, I used to think that confidence was a King's Road state of mind, but, the older I get, the more I realize that confidence can be copied, and it's perfectly possible to fake it to make it. Or, rather, if you start by pretending to be confident, it seeps into your soul and becomes the real deal.

Being confident isn't about being loud. Some of the most fascinating people I know are the ones who don't yell for attention, they somehow command it with their stillness and self-possession. In fact, so many people think that they need to make a lot of noise in order to be seen and heard, but your confidence won't be convincing unless it's based on who you are. If you're not naturally noisy, don't think that you have to show off or act up. You won't impress anyone, you'll just be exhausted. Mark-Francis is one of the most confident people I know, and he would *never* do most of the things we often associate with confidence. I couldn't imagine him dancing on a table or singing karaoke – or even raising his voice above five decibels. Yet, he's the King of Confidence, and I think this is because he's constantly true to himself and he genuinely enjoys his own company. In the nicest possible way, he makes you feel as though his time is a gift that he's bestowing upon you because you're worth it. So, an hour with Mark makes *you* feel confident, too, even when he's got some fairly frank things to say about your shoes.

Ultimately, I think confidence is about self-belief and finding your place as a person in the world. You need to embrace the idea that you're no better or worse than anyone else and stop worrying about satisfying your ego. It's not about feeling that you're the most important person in the room. It's about making sure that, no matter which room you're in, you know that you have just as much right to be there as anyone else.

Interesting people are interested people – ask lots of questions

Insecurity is the enemy of confidence, and I think nothing makes us feel more insecure than the fear of not knowing the answer. Think about the first time you questioned your confidence and felt a bit wobbly. For me, it was being at school and getting grilled by my maths teacher on the finer points of long division. I felt so stressed and pressured that my brain went blank, and the harder I tried to think of an answer – any answer – the more frightened I felt. Sometimes, I see people at parties being really boring about their specialist subjects, and I realize that they're not nearly as confident as they seem. They're trying to mask it by proving they're clever enough to retain information, just in case their maths teacher has been invited and suddenly forces them to divide 892 by 327. We simply can't know everything about everything, and this fact makes our confidence falter. There's only one way to fight this: instead of attempting to be the person who has all the answers, be the person who asks all the questions!

Firstly, most people are quite vain, and if you treat them as though they're knowledgeable and intelligent, they'll be flattered by your interest and assume that's an indication of your own cleverness. Also, admitting that you don't know something is a bit of a bold move. It suggests that you genuinely don't care what people think of you, which gives you extra confidence points. Men like my friend Stanley spend a lot of time with other men in their seventies, who never ask questions of each other, because they all assume they know everything. If you ask these guys a question, they're delighted, because they rarely get to show off their knowledge without some other seventy-year-old trying to speak over them!

Be charming – and disarming

Lots of people think charm is a bit old-fashioned, but I couldn't disagree more. This isn't about perfecting a curtsey, or learning which order to use your forks in, although those are fun things to know. You never know when they'll come in useful! I even charmed Prince Charles once! I was standing in the receiving line with a group of people when he visited the *This Morning* studios. When he shook my hand, I blurted out, 'Don't worry! I didn't bring back anything nasty from the jungle!' He laughed a

> ❝ Whether you're sashaying to a date in a cocktail frock or wearing your favourite jacket to a big meeting, making an effort on the outside will make you feel much better on the inside. ❞

lot, and I heard that he wanted to stay and chat some more. Your Royal Highness, if you're reading this, I'm *always* available!

Charm is about working out how to put other people at their ease, while making sure they remember you and enjoy your company. It's a tricky ratio of politeness, friendliness, funniness and respect. You need to tailor your charm and deploy it in an appropriate way. There's a kind you use at work and a very different sort you use on dates.

Charm is an important part of confidence, because being charming is connected with believing at your very core that everyone you meet is going to be pleased to see you. This sounds quite arrogant, but if you're feeling nervous, it's very soothing.

Before I went into the jungle, I really wanted to charm everyone I met when I was out there. This was because I didn't expect them to like me on sight, and I knew that I had to show them the positive parts of my personality, simply because that would make the whole experience much more pleasant for everyone. I think charm is the opposite of what Marilyn Monroe is supposed to have said – that people should be able to handle her at her worst, or they don't deserve her at her best. No offence to Marilyn, but this is nonsense! I'm not at my best every single day, but I make a real effort to try, because I know the world is a much nicer place when we're all kind, funny and *fun*!

I used to think that charm was about letting creepy guys kiss your hand or being able to make small talk with a duchess. This isn't the case. Charm is smiling at a stranger and telling her you love her bag. It's laughing loudly when your shyest auntie reads the terrible joke from her Christmas cracker. It's making eye contact and saying thank you to every waiter, taxi driver and hair stylist you meet, and leaving a tip. It's about letting your best friend tell her favourite story to the boy she's trying to impress, without joining in with the punchline. It's about believing in your very best self and getting a boost from seeing it reflected back by the world.

Enthusiasm goes a long way

Unfairly, lots of people who struggle with confidence are dismissed for being rude, when, really, they're quite shy. These people hold back because they're not sure how to join in, and everyone thinks they're aloof and grumpy. Sometimes, I wonder whether the character Mr Darcy really was as arrogant and self-assured as he seemed, or whether there's a backstory where he fell on his arse during a school assembly and spent the rest of his life trying to live it down, with his hands folded behind his back.

Bearing this in mind, it's worth knowing that enthusiasm is one of the fastest ways to fake confidence. Everything exciting in my life has happened because I said, 'Yes!' I'll admit that sometimes this has gone against my better judgement. Sure, there were occasional moments in the jungle when my brain was telling me to run screaming from the cockroaches and demand a flight straight home. There were even moments when I was in LA, covering the Oscars for *This Morning*, when I wished I was five thousand miles away and under my duvet. Especially when I missed my cue and the cameras caught me looking slightly jet-lagged! Still, even though it didn't go perfectly, I'm so glad I embraced the opportunity, and I'd definitely do it again. If I waited until I felt absolutely ready to try everything that I get asked to do, I'd never do anything. I'd probably still be cleaning the loo in my dad's office. Being excited and positive about life forces you to be confident, in the same way that signing up for a charity 5K forces you to get fit. It's not about winning the race – you only need to get around the course – and, in both cases, you'll probably discover that you're much more prepared than you realize.

Take pride in your appearance

Confidence comes from feeling good, and if you want to feel good, you need to look good, too. It's OK to be a little bit vain. The way you actually look doesn't matter at all, but there's a real blast of confidence that comes from putting your best face forward.

Think about pantomime dames. They are usually incredibly confident characters and, while they don't wear outfits that we might go for, they're loud, proud and seemingly invincible, and part of their power seems to come from wearing eight different kinds of fabric embellished with clashing neon sequins. *RuPaul's Drag Race* is total fashion inspiration, even if you're more of a classic dresser, like me. (I think my drag name would have to be something like 'Taupe DeLine' and RuPaul would tell me off for not putting enough ass in my pastel.) Every contestant on that show demonstrates that there's a clear connection between confidence and appearance, and they seem to draw energy from their wardrobe.

Whether you're sashaying to a date in a cocktail frock or wearing your favourite jacket to a big meeting, making an effort on the outside will make you feel much better on the inside. I firmly believe this is why everyone in Chelsea is so addicted to blow-dries. If all of the hair salons shut down overnight, Chelsea would be eighty per cent less confident. The stock market would probably crash.

For me, as you know, my concealer is my magical confidence wand. I feel so much more optimistic about my day if I know that the Estée Lauder Double Wear is in my bag. If you've got a favourite part of your appearance, emphasize it, and if something makes you feel self-conscious, find a way of making sure that it doesn't come between you and your positive vibes. Remember, there are no rules. Loads of people have told me that red lipstick is their secret weapon, but it just makes me look as though I've had my face painted at a school fete.

Toughen up

If you want to be more confident, it really helps to start by becoming resilient. I can be super sensitive about certain things, and completely fine about others. I think it's normal to have really strong moments and then moments where you feel more fragile than a soggy box of Kleenex. Some days, I feel as though I could win the Nobel Prize by lunchtime, and, on others, a savage Insta comment will bring me to my knees. Perspective makes me stronger. Occasionally, I need to give myself a good talking to, in order to make sure I don't wallow and that I remember how great my life really is.

We all know that we're much more critical of ourselves than we'd ever be towards any of our friends. It's really important to be kind to ourselves, but it's also helpful to channel the negative voice and use it to make ourselves feel a bit tougher. Sometimes, I remember my old cadets training and think about how challenging I found every task – and how good I felt when I managed to succeed. Similarly, the jungle was the toughest experience of my life, and there were moments when I felt much too sensitive to carry on. I had to push myself as hard as I could, and I'm so proud of myself for not giving up. It's always worth going through a difficult challenge, because you're bound to be much more confident when you come out the other side. You're capable of much more than you ever imagined.

Enjoy your own company

For me, this has been one of the hardest lessons to learn. You can't be confident if you're needy. In my experience, the people who attract friends and admirers are the ones who are brilliant at being self-reliant. I adore being in big groups, and I think I'm naturally a true extrovert in that I draw a lot of my energy from being around other people. However, if you can learn to feel as though you're enough when you're alone, you'll appreciate your friends more, because they're a bonus. You can be with them because you want to be; you're not hoping that they'll complete you. This is really important in romantic relationships, too. The people I know who are great at being by themselves are the ones who tend to keep their cool, and they don't rush into anything they regret. The people who don't enjoy their own company have a tendency to overthink things and obsess about where the relationship is going, which only makes them miserable.

I don't think that we live in a world which encourages us to be by ourselves – or even to like ourselves. It's extremely difficult to stay confident if your alone time is spent scrolling your way through social media. If you're anything like me, you'll get horrible, terrible FOMO, along with a nagging sense that nothing is as it seems, and nothing is worth doing if people aren't liking it. If I'm constantly checking to see who has retweeted my joke, and whether anyone is trolling me, I'm not spending quality time with myself, I'm just chipping away at my confidence. If you're here reading, you're doing the right thing. Books are the only friends that can actually help you to become good at enjoying your alone time.

Keep a sense of perspective

Nothing makes you feel less confident than the fear that everyone is better than you – and nothing makes you more unpleasant than believing that you're better than everyone else. The key to true confidence is to remember that, broadly speaking, you're doing fine, and success can only be measured by how much you enjoy what you do. It's great to be inspired by people, but there's no point in getting too competitive if it's making you feel jealous, nervous and sad. Besides, life tends to move at such a fast pace that the person you envy right now will probably wish they were doing what you're doing in a couple of months. If you look too hard at other people's lives, you'll miss out on your own, or, as Oscar Wilde said, 'Be yourself. Everyone else is already taken.' Confidence comes from being glad that you're *you*.

Show, don't tell

Once you've started to master the art of confidence, you'll realize that people are responding to you in a slightly different way. It will suddenly become clear to the world that you know exactly who you are and where you're going, and you don't need to explain yourself or your talents – they will be obvious to everyone watching.

Ironically, this is the biggest difference between a confident person and a show-off. Show-offs don't 'show' at all. They tell people about every single one of their activities and achievements, right down to the swimming certificate they were awarded when they were seven. These people would be slightly more interesting to listen to if they read out the Yellow Pages instead. Don't fall into this trap. When you feel confident, you'll realize that you don't need to prove yourself to anyone or wait to be seen and approved of. Confidence is all about quietly getting on with it, and truly believing that you're doing a good job.

The secret is – there's no secret!

I used to believe that some people were born confident, or that there was a meeting somewhere about how to seem incredibly self-assured at all times, and I missed it because I left the house too late and was stuck in the back of a taxi while everyone else was learning the secrets of the universe. Now, I know that I didn't realize how confident I was until something happened to shake my sense of self. My early teen years were so tricky because the bullies had shaken my confidence badly, and I didn't know how to go back to the way I felt before. The most confident people I've met haven't lived charmed lives. They don't know a trick or a hack that makes them feel better than everyone else. The one thing they all have in common is that they have encountered adversity and come out the other side. The only real secret of confidence is that you'll only realize how important it is when something in your life shakes it, and makes you worry about who you are. You can only be truly confident if you've endured a challenge. Once you know where confidence comes from, you'll realize that no one is naturally more confident than you are. They just truly believe that, although bad things might happen to them, brilliant things will come along too.

Quick confidence boosters! How to start the day with a smile on your face

Put on your special-occasion perfume!
You know, the one you save for dates and the days when you might bump into your ex. It will give you a boost, and you'll trick your brain into looking forward to what's in store.

Embrace being late
If you're not going to be on time, rushing probably won't get you anywhere. It might even make you later, because you'll end up dropping cereal down your dress, or getting halfway down the road with no money or keys. Lean into your lateness and relax! Feeling bad won't save time. Sometimes, when I'm on the bus, I think of a really creative excuse to entertain the person I'm late

171

for. They won't believe me, but they might forgive me if I can make them laugh.

Start your day with some classical music

You can pretend to be a mature, sophisticated person as you sip your herbal tea, and you'll feel calm and prepared. It's so much more relaxing than reading Twitter on your phone in bed and finding out about who has threatened to blow up whom in the night. It's much easier to feel confident when you're not constantly contemplating when and how the world might end.

Spend some time with Mark-Francis!

Or, if he's not available, your most confident friend, and find out about the one part of their daily routine that they would never skip. Although, I think the word 'routine' would make Mark shudder and heave. Some people need black coffee, silence and fifty pages of a difficult French novel. Some need their Spotify Tropical House playlist and a glass of Nesquik. It might take some time to discover what works for you, but you can have fun finding out!

Promise yourself a 'no'

I *hate* saying no to anyone, and I think 'yes' is the word of fun and opportunity, but sometimes a 'no' is a really useful voucher. You need to be able to say it in order to establish your boundaries and make sure that people don't take advantage of your good nature. Essentially, this is great for confidence because, if you remember that you have a right to say no, you're reminding yourself that nothing bad is going to happen to you, because no one is going to make you do anything that makes you feel unhappy or uncomfortable. You're in charge!

A letter to my fourteen-year-old self

Dear Georgia,

Your teens are confusing, and, at the moment, you're trying to figure out who you are, where you belong, and what's important to you. The very first thing I want to tell you is that you've got this. You don't know what lies ahead of you, but you don't need to worry about anything. Right now, you're as confident as you'll ever be. Celebrate it! You're full of energy, and you'll embrace every adventure that comes your way. Never lose that spirit, because that's more important than any exam or bit of wisdom. Your enthusiasm is your greatest asset. However, exams and grades are important, and sometimes people make you feel as though it isn't cool to care. You're smart, you like school and you want to do well. This isn't anything to be ashamed of. On the contrary, you should be proud of the fact that you're a bit of a nerd. In the future, you'll realize that there's never any reason to hide your intelligence. Working hard leads to great things. Ignore anyone who makes you feel as though you shouldn't be pleased with your grades, or that it isn't OK to try hard. They're not on the same path as you. One day, young girls will be looking up to you, and you'll want them to embrace the opportunities they have at school. Try your best to do the same.

However, while your teachers can't fault your work, they do have some problems with your uniform – or, rather, your interpretation of the uniform. Please brush your hair. I know that this is the look right now, and everyone looks as though so many birds are nesting on their head that David Attenborough might turn up with a camera crew – but you'll look back and wonder why you basically let your hair turn into dreadlocks. Think about your poor biology teacher, who keeps sending you out of the classroom with a comb. Don't just slowly walk back to your boarding house, and then come back with the same hair. It's an insult to his intelligence and yours. Also, don't laugh, but, in about five years, you'll be obsessed with blow-dries and hot rollers. Keep your hair in good condition and you'll be glad you did.

While we're here, can you please be a bit more chill with the bronzer? I know that everyone loves caking their face in shimmery powder, but you'll look back at old photos and wonder why you always look as though you have poo on your face. Right now, you have beautiful skin – one day, you'll feel much more self-conscious about it, and you'll wish that you showed it off when you could! Dealing with your skin is going to be tough, and, although you can't imagine it now, it will make you feel insecure and self-conscious as you enter the adult world. However, when you open up about your skincare struggles, you'll inspire thousands of women who face similar problems, and this will make you feel amazing. Also, never, ever let anyone make you feel bad about wanting to put concealer on from the second that you wake up. This is your inalienable right!

There's nothing wrong with caring about your appearance. As a junior cadet, you will constantly be called out for not having the right uniform, wearing too much make-up and, once again, not brushing your hair or tying it back. Your poor platoon will constantly be doing extra push-ups as a punishment, because of your endless uniform infringements.

Here are a few hacks that you'll wish you'd known a bit earlier on. If you rub some Vaseline on your boots, they'll look as though you've been polishing them for hours and hours. Ironing a crease in your combat trousers takes ages, but if you've forgotten to sort out your laundry, you can quickly make a fake crease with a pair of hair straighteners. Most importantly, your eccentric style will be rewarded when you're given the Combat Barbie award at the end of the course! That's quite an accolade! Of course, Combat Barbie will eventually become Jungle Barbie, and everything you've learned as a cadet will be incredibly useful to you when you're dealing with snakes and food rationing.

Being a cadet is difficult, but you're learning about endurance and discovering that you might be little, but you can be incredibly tough when you put your mind to it. The experience will also show you that you need to stay true to yourself. In some situations, you'll feel as though you don't fit in straight away, but it's your differences that are your strengths, not doing the same thing as everyone else. Right now, you're making friends who will be in your life for a long time, as well as discovering what you're like as a friend, and what you need from your friends.

Most of your best mates are boys, and you feel a bit self-conscious about this. When you look around, it seems as though every other girl at school has lots of really close girlfriends, and you feel sad and excluded. Don't worry. All that matters is the way that your friends make you feel, and you've not failed because most of your best friends are boys. When you're a bit older, you'll have the most brilliant gang of guys in your life, and you'll be closer to them than anyone you've ever met. Being friends with boys means that you can escape some of the bitchiness and competitiveness that you've noticed from some of the other girls. However, don't discount female friends. Puberty is difficult for everyone, and you'll meet some brilliant women in the future, when you've all come out the other side.

> ❛ The jungle was the toughest experience of my life, and there were moments where I felt much too sensitive to carry on. ❜

You're still getting over some really awful bullying. A couple of years ago, you dealt with one of the toughest, most painful experiences imaginable, when that group of girls was so cruel, so frequently, that you ended up moving schools. You'll never really understand what made them do that, or why they chose you as a target. However, in the future, you'll realize that bullies are never happy. Hurt people hurt people, and those girls must have been desperately insecure and in a lot of pain to make you feel the way they did. Being friends with boys makes you feel safe – you've never seen them pick on people this way. However, you're about to make a friend who will change your life.

When Amy turns up in your dorm, you will hate her on sight and wonder why this random girl is invading your space. But she'll become your best friend within about twenty-four hours. Amy is amazing. She's one of the best people you'll ever meet, and she'll save your life every single day. If it wasn't for her, you probably wouldn't ever make it down for breakfast. You and Amy have different skills, and you'll complement each other. She'll teach you how to notice when someone needs help, and how to ask when you need a metaphorical leg-up. You and Amy will end up on slightly different journeys, as she travels the world on a yacht and you travel to the Australian jungle with Ant and Dec. There will come a time when you'll have to wait for months to see each other, so treasure these years when you see each other almost every day – even when she throws a sausage roll at your head. (You'll never remember what the fight was about, but you'll always remember how it felt to watch the sausage roll flying through the air, before it hit you in the face.) Also, Amy will teach you that it's the little things that matter. You will never buy anyone a gift that is as appreciated as the McDonald's hash brown you bring her on a Friday morning, on your way from the bus stop.

Another person who will be in your life forever is Mikey. You're both young, but you and Mikey really love each other. He'll bring out your inner daredevil. Years later, you won't be able to explain quite how you found the guts to sneak into his room in Harrow and hide in the wardrobe. For one thing, that's quite a difficult school to get into! You needed to be extremely stealthy in order to thwart security! Right now, you think that you're like Romeo and Juliet, only with less tragedy and more begging your parents for phone credit. There will come a day when Mikey breaks your heart, at the barriers of Victoria station, while you beg him to change his mind and stay with you. A few years later, in December, you'll be driving him home for Christmas, singing along to Chris Rea!

Getting over Mikey will be hard, and you won't really be able to talk to him for about a year, but keep the faith. You'll get there, and, when you do, you'll be so happy that he's still your friend and that you can love each other so much without being romantically involved. I wish I could go back and stop you from making a huge mistake and binning all of the lovely presents and letters that Mikey gave you – especially the tank top he made you that said, *You're gorgeous!* because you both loved the Babybird song of the same name. If time travel is invented in our lifetime, we need to make sure we rescue this.

There will be times when you think that boys are exciting, mysterious creatures that know the secrets of the universe. You'll get over this pretty quickly. I have two words for you – Tom Ricketts. Right now, he's the fittest guy in the whole school. Sometimes, you and your friends are late for lessons because you spot him somewhere and need to stop for a good gaze. Tom Ricketts seems like a distant sex god. But, in five years, you'll be snogging him in a club in Oxford! I did this for you, teenage Toff, because I knew how excited you'd be, if you could only know what's going to happen! Now, Tom isn't this cool, remote film-star hottie. He's a mate. He's also still pretty good looking!

While we're here, we need to talk about FOMO. At the moment, you're so desperate to be in the middle of everything that it's interfering with your sleep. You'll stay up all night and power through until the next day before you'll miss a single second of anything, whether it's school, gossip or fun. This is going to get worse before it gets better. If you think you're glued to your phone now, in a few years' time, it will be surgically attached to your hand. Instagram and WhatsApp don't rule your life yet, but beware! I know it sounds insane, but you'll be able to see pictures of every single party that happens each weekend, including the ones you can't go to. Try to make peace with the fact that you're a human being who needs at least eight hours of sleep a night, and who can only physically be in one place at a time. Some nights, you'll need to stay in. That's OK. It's better to go out a few times and really enjoy it, than to go out constantly and have a so-so time. There will always be another party to go to, and you'll enjoy it more if you're occasionally in bed by eleven.

Over the next few years, politics will start to play a bigger part in your life. Being informed and opinionated really matters to you, and you're going to start becoming really passionate about current affairs and understanding what is happening in the wider world. This is going to be a life-long love affair. Embrace it! Get as geeky as you dare! Learn as much as you can, and don't be afraid to go to events and ask loads of questions. However, do remember that, occasionally, what you say may come back to bite you on the bottom, and, even when you're joking, some people will take your comments very seriously. You may, at some point, regret calling a senior politician a 'sex god' and then having to apologize to his wife. However, if you can laugh this off, you can deal with anything!

Even though you sometimes feel anxious and insecure, right now you're almost fearless. Also, you're really good at living in the moment. You're discovering how to have fun, surrounding yourself with the people who make you happy, and working out what your values are. Most importantly, you're learning how to stay true to them and be your authentic self. You're quietly confident, and you have a natural energy and positivity that draws people to you. Right now, your life is fairly easy; in the future, it might become slightly more difficult. There's nothing to be scared of. That's all part of growing up. But, as you learn to take care of yourself and start to become more independent, you might find yourself becoming more cautious, and increasingly aware of your own vulnerabilities. That's totally natural, but I want you to promise that you'll never forget about the girl you are right now: the girl who says 'yes', who rushes into rooms beaming; the girl who always sees the upside and realizes that the more challenging the opportunity seems, the more exciting it could become.

You're going to be presented with more opportunities than you ever thought possible. You'll see the world, be on T.V., get sent free clothes and meet your heroes. People will recognize you in Waitrose, while you're buying loo roll. This is going to be every bit as weird and amazing as it sounds. Be proud and excited!

Seize every chance you have, and enjoy the ride. But, also, don't be afraid to step back from it every so often. Try to be with your family and friends, and the people who truly know you, not just the ones who think they do. You're going to become a role model for many women. Think about what's important to you right now. While lots of people will want to copy you because they like your clothes or your lifestyle, remember that those are all fun extras – and that the most important thing is always to be kind. It's cool to be kind, and you must remember to be kind to yourself, too.

Finally, promise me that you'll enjoy everything. You're going to make mistakes. You're always going to look back at your life and occasionally wish you hadn't bought that dress, or that you'd gone to a different party, or didn't kiss that boy. You can only regret what you don't do, and if you never get it wrong, you won't learn anything. You're going to have so much fun. Enjoy every second.

Lots of love,

You

Standing Up For Yourself

I had an odd conversation with a chap at a dinner party once.

'You're quite opinionated, aren't you?' he said, as I mused on European policy while we waited for pudding.

'I'm sorry, what?' I replied. I thought we were just chatting, but, apparently, he wasn't used to talking to people who disagreed with him – especially women.

Of course I'm opinionated – who isn't?! Everyone who has a favourite flavour of crisps or an objection to painting their bathroom bright green is holding an opinion. Yet, even though we have a female Prime Minister, some people are still surprised when they meet intelligent women who have strong views and beliefs, and simply expect us to smile at them and nod along, like those dogs people put in the back of the car. I say, 'No more!' If I can encourage young women to do one thing, I hope it's to be proud of their opinions and, more importantly, not to be shy about sharing them.

The trouble is that, when you're blonde, short and posh, no one is really expecting you to stand up for yourself. Even the kindest, most thoughtful people tend to assume you're a bit of a bimbo, until you get talking. While I'm aware that the way I look and speak brings me all kinds of privileges and advantages, and I'm deeply fortunate, I also know that, if I were a taller, spectacle-wearing brunette, it would be slightly easier for me to, say, talk politics on *Newsnight*, and have people at least listen to what I was saying without immediately writing me off as an idiot. To be honest, this is why I make the 'Jungle Barbie' joke – if I make the joke before anyone else does, it shows that I'm slightly self-aware!

However, I also think my biggest advantage is this: when I share my opinions and debate the subjects that I'm passionate about, I can bring an element of surprise. People who don't know me very well don't realize that I feel so strongly, particularly about politics, and they're simply not expecting these thoughts to come out of my mouth. It's easier than it sounds, and I think that the world is full of deeply intelligent young women who don't speak up, simply because they've been made to feel as though they'll be laughed at, or at least not listened to, if they say what's on their mind.

Ever since I started talking about politics, I've realized that the subject comes up at every event and interview. I think this is because there aren't that many young women in my position who are willing to open up and talk about it publically, because they're worried about being laughed at or shouted down. The fact that

I do discuss it has become my calling card. I think that political parties on either side of the debate would do so much better if they encouraged everyone to take an interest, and made it clear that it doesn't matter what your job is, or where you went to school, you can get involved if you want to.

Learning to stand up for yourself is a vital life skill, and it's probably one of the toughest, most valuable lessons I learned at school. The most extreme example happened when I was being bullied. At the time, I found it impossible to stand up to the girls who were bullying me. If people have decided to be cruel and unkind, it's extremely difficult to change their minds with intelligent debate. The bullying shook my confidence to its core. However, afterwards, I realized there were two ways I could react. I could spend the rest of my life lurking in the shadows, feeling terrified about drawing attention to myself and hoping that no one would ever notice me again. Or, I could decide that the worst thing that could happen had just happened, and I didn't have anything to gain from keeping my mouth closed. Bullies are less likely to go for confident people – and, if I became more confident about who I was and what I had to say, hopefully I'd never be picked on again.

It was around this time that I started to take an interest in politics. When I was fourteen, I became a member of the Conservative party, because I started to feel very strongly about what was happening in the country, and how it was being run. Broadly speaking, I think that most of the people I have grown up with have fairly similar views to mine. However, I'd say that most of my friends aren't actively political. They have thoughts and opinions, but not necessarily a space to voice them. No one ever really asks them what they're thinking, so they don't get a chance to really formulate their views.

There have been two major occasions where I've been challenged by people whose views are the direct opposite of mine. Instead of just having a noisy debate in the pub, where everyone starts out intensely and then gets distracted after ordering chips, I was on T.V., up against people who wanted to debate me and win. I met the left-wing political campaigner and food blogger Jack Monroe, and then a boy called Benjie, who I was set up with on *Celebs Go Dating*. Opposites did not attract.

I really adored having the chance to speak to Jack. She held an entirely different set of opinions to mine, but she debated with such sensitivity and intelligence that I really wanted to think seriously about what she had to say, and she changed my mind about some of the beliefs and values that were already in my head. She really opened my eyes to what it means to be privileged, and the fact that so many people are struggling and need support. I think we were both surprised to discover how much we had in common, and the fact that, while we have some big differences, the similarities were there, too. Most importantly, she was kind and compassionate. Even though we're coming from such different places, I felt as though we could be respectful of each other and enjoy each other's company.

This is why it's so important to learn to speak about what you care about. A proper, non-shouty debate is so useful. Usually, I don't spend that much time with people who hold opposing views to mine, and, when I do, it often descends into a shouting match, which means that everyone comes away feeling furious and no one learns anything. Which is exactly what happened to me on *Celebs Go Dating*.

When someone describes themselves as being 'hideously left wing', it's probably clear from the start that we were never meant to hit it off. I don't think Benjie was interested in sensibly discussing our differences. He said he believed in equal opportunities for everyone, and I do, too. But he was so negative! I really wish that we could have had a proper debate, but it seemed he was determined to dismiss me because I'm posh and privileged. Because he was so argumentative, I didn't handle the date as well as I would have liked to. It was so frustrating. Firstly, I was genuinely hoping that I might just meet a nice boy that I wanted to see again. I'm not sure that dating was really on his agenda at all. I think it's really important to learn to stay calm and keep being open-minded. When you speak your mind, there are people who will go out of their way to push your buttons, and that's something that you need to prepare for. But it's hard! If you've ever watched *Question*

> ❛ If I can encourage young women to do one thing, I hope it's to be proud of their opinions and, more importantly, not to be shy about sharing them. ❜

189

Time, or tuned in to what's going on in the House of Commons, you'll know that even seasoned politicians have a hard time when it comes to keeping their cool.

For me, being a Conservative is all about encouraging and rewarding hard work, but of course there's much more to it than that – and I'm aware that plenty of people disagree with me. At school, my teachers were keen to ask me what my opinions were, and challenge them, which gave me lots of practice. They taught me that standing up for yourself isn't just about saying what you think. It's about learning as much as you possibly can in order to qualify and explain your beliefs, and so your thoughts are informed. You need to back your feelings up with facts. This doesn't just apply to politics. In fact, that's really just the beginning of the challenge. Whether you want to talk about books, art, or what you want for lunch, being able to express yourself and your desires will take you far in life.

However, I know that many people don't have that experience at school. If your teachers take an interest in what you say, you're really lucky. Some of us have to learn how to express our opinions later in life. There's always time to figure this out, and I've got some tips. I'm still learning.

Learn how to debate

Before I started following politics, I used to think that you had to be some kind of magician in order to debate properly. However, now that I've observed some successful debates, and some bad ones, I realize that there are a few very simple tricks that will take you far. Firstly, debating tends to attract the most competitive, overconfident people you will ever meet. These are people who will happily spend hours explaining why you're wrong to put lime in your gin and tonic, when you could have a slice of lemon. They don't care about citrus fruit; they just want to win.

Once you realize that you're in the presence of someone who loves to, ahem, mass debate, don't throw yourself straight into the fray. Watch them closely and see what you notice about their technique. At least ninety-five per cent of it will be acting. If you analyse their facts and figures, a quick google might show you that the statistics they're pulling out of the air aren't necessarily true, but they state them with such confidence that no one questions them. Most importantly, these debaters have stamina. Nothing and no one can interrupt them.

You'll notice that many of these debates happen after lunch, when everyone is back from the loo. It's impossible to debate properly on an empty stomach, or while you need a wee. I think Jamie Laing is the king of this sort of debate, because he has endless energy. He's like the Duracell Bunny of disagreeing with people. However, one thing to watch out for is the fact that most of these debates aren't won by people because they have made a series of brilliant and irrefutable points. It's because everyone else gets so bored and tired that they give up, and the debater wins by sheer focus and willpower.

Do your research

When it comes to speaking your mind, facts are your best friends. This can be political, and involve information about employment statistics, money spent on public health or interest rates, but it can also be useful on a more personal level. If you and your friends are arguing about where to go on holiday, learn about local temperatures, exchange rates and how much beer you can buy for a fiver. That way, your argument will hold much more weight than your friend's, when they wave their phone in your face and tell you that they want to go to rural Poland in February because they've seen a really pretty picture on Instagram.

The other brilliant thing about research is that sometimes you discover new facts and end up changing your mind. That's fine. Speaking out and standing up for yourself isn't about holding on to one viewpoint and refusing to think about anything else, ever. It's about doing what feels right and logical, and sometimes that means adapting to change. For example, discovering that Poland actually has some really beautiful architecture, and extremely reasonably priced vodka.

Be passionate – but keep a cool head

Passion is the entire point of speaking your mind. There is no point in saying what you think unless you really, really care about it. That said, if we've learned anything from the professional debaters, it's that it's often easier to keep banging on about something if you don't care. When you're talking about anything that matters to you, you need a little bit of distance and perspective. For example, I love pop music with all my heart, and I'm really not bothered about R & B. It's not my thing at all. So, if I was with someone who was challenging my belief that cheesy music is the best music, I might struggle to keep my emotions in check. What I'd need to do is say that, in the UK, the longest-running number one in the last twenty years was Bryan Adams' 'Everything I Do (I Do It For You)', which is pure cheese – and Bryan beat Drake by a couple of weeks. Apparently, this is a much more compelling argument than shouting, 'You're wrong! How *dare* you!' and bursting into tears before demanding another glass of white wine.

However, don't forget that your passion and excitement will make people listen to you. If you're bored by what you're talking about, you'll sound boring. Your enthusiasm is your greatest asset. It makes you sparky and fascinating. Think about how persuasive people can be when they love their subject matter so much that they come alive before your eyes! This is why Mary Beard is brilliant. She's one of the cleverest people on the planet, and, when she speaks, you know that she loves her job so much that you can't help but listen. You catch more flies with honey, and when you're positive, enthusiastic and genuine, people will think it's really sweet. Usually, arguments are associated with anger, but passion and joy can be so much more powerful and persuasive. If you know exactly why you love something, you're in a position to make other people care about it, too – or, at least, to see the situation from your point of view.

Play to your strengths

When it comes to speaking out and saying what's on your mind, it makes sense to lean into what you're good at. As I said, not everyone takes me seriously because I can come across like a bit of a bimbo. I'm young, I'm blonde and I wear a lot of pink. Still, like Elle Woods in *Legally Blonde*, I know that there is no point in me pretending to be someone I'm not, just to get people to listen to me. This is partly because it would probably backfire. You can't convince anyone to respect your beliefs if they think you're hiding something or trying to be someone else. Embracing who you are and what you're good at will give you a much more solid platform when it comes to speaking up.

If you're naturally quiet, you don't have to shout to make yourself heard. When it seems as though everyone around you is yelling over each other, you can be much more interesting and compelling if you embrace your quietness and force people to stop what they're doing and really focus to hear you. If you feel unsure, and you're not comfortable making big statements, try to

6 If I was with someone who was challenging my belief that cheesy music is the best music, I might struggle to keep my emotions in check. 9

get your point across by asking lots of questions. If someone has said something that you fundamentally disagree with, you don't have to challenge them with a fact. You can ask them, kindly and politely, to talk you through their logic and reasoning. You'll either learn something or prove them wrong with your curiosity! My favourite people are brilliant at using humour in a wicked way during a debate. Mark-Francis is so good at this. Someone can talk nonsense for hours, and he can counter their opinion with a devastating put-down and a well-timed Oscar Wilde quotation.

Believe in yourself

Speaking your mind can be such a struggle if you're feeling nervous or insecure about yourself. It's easy to compare yourself to other people and assume that you're up against people who are much cleverer or more quick-witted than you are. This is nonsense. The only difference between you and the people who feel comfortable about voicing their opinions is confidence. If you've watched debates, either in Parliament or over the dinner table, you'll be aware that plenty of people suffer from overconfidence, and they are expressing a different kind of insecurity by daring people to disagree with them.

However, all you need to know is that you have as much right to express yourself as anyone else, and no one has the right to speak over you. If people think you're too shy and nervous to speak up, they might try to take advantage of you and bully you

195

into agreeing with them. Yet, if you can take a deep breath and a big gulp of courage, you'll probably find that you can shock them into listening, simply because you dared to share an independent thought.

Also, it's good to know that speaking out makes you more confident, and it gets slightly easier every time you do it. Find tiny opportunities to share. Volunteer to do some public speaking at a work presentation or talk to friends about news stories that have inspired you to think more deeply about particular subjects. You can share thoughts on social media – it's slightly less scary than it might be in real life, although you can guarantee that you'll find someone who is desperate to disagree with the most straightforward statement. I think that we all have moments when we can't avoid speaking out. If we can prepare with a few practice runs, we're much more likely to do it well when we need to. At least, we should be able to avoid any fear-based vomiting.

Agree to disagree

The most important part of speaking up for yourself is that you feel better and braver for saying what's on your mind. Not all arguments need to be won, and sometimes you simply have to embrace everyone's differences and call it a draw. The writer Evelyn Beatrice Hall is famous for the line, 'I do not agree with what you have to say, but I'll defend to the death your right to say it.' It's really important to remember this when you get caught up in an argument. If I do get swept away by a passionate debate, I always try to be respectful of the person I'm debating with and make an effort to remember that it's not about the fact that I think I'm right, which makes them wrong. If they haven't been persuaded by my points, I need to try to understand why they believe in theirs. Usually, there are at least two sides to every argument, idea and point of view. The world would be horribly boring if we all agreed all the time. I wish more people in politics were better at this. It's always better to have a respectful debate than an all-out war!

Fashion and Style

When you live in Chelsea, it's easy to find yourself wearing a sort of uniform. This can be very handy when you're running late and standing in front of your wardrobe in your knickers, staring at a sea of sequins and wondering what to do. Honestly, the only thing that stops me going out for breakfast in a ballgown is that no one would believe that I wasn't still wearing it from the night before. Anyway, if you need to look sensible and you're absolutely stuck, simply follow the Chelsea dress code and you're ready to go absolutely everywhere. During the day, all you need is clean jeans, a smart jacket – perhaps a bit of faux fur, or a nice blazer – boots, a shirt and, if it's a cold day and you're really keen to commit to the aesthetic, a hat. Ideally, you want some kind of fedora. Don't simply google 'Chelsea hat' and buy something on the Internet, unless you're a committed football supporter.

The best thing about the 'uniform' is that it creates a style democracy. You can look good in it whether you're eighteen or eighty, it suits all body types and it doesn't fluctuate too much with fashion. As long as your boots don't have *2015!* sprayed down the side in gold letters, you can get years of wear out of them. However, while it's easy to personalize and customize the look, you'd probably get a bit bored if you wore it every single day. It doesn't fit with my personal fashion philosophy, which is really very similar to my general life philosophy: have fun, try lots of new things and don't be afraid to take a few risks!

It's very difficult to live in Chelsea and not turn into a total shopaholic. You're constantly surrounded by exciting, shiny new things, window displays change every week and, best of all, you know that, no matter what you buy, you'll always be able to find an occasion to show it off. It's a bit like living in the middle of a magazine – only, magazines don't show pictures of people who can't shut their wardrobes, or beds with legs that don't quite touch the ground because so many bags have been stowed beneath them. The sheer amount of *stuff* that you accumulate is quite scary, and I've been trying my hardest to get slightly better at reusing, recycling and making trips to my local Red Cross charity shops to donate some of the more bonkers bits of my wardrobe. You know, the things you see and wonder, What was I thinking? Oh, yeah – I'd had half a bottle of wine and decided that Big Bird was my all-time fashion icon. The trouble with donating to charity shops is that it's very easy to come back with bags filled with new finds, and you end up with more stuff than you started with. Still, it's all for a very good cause.

One important thing to tell you is that, while the Chelsea 'look' is definitely pretty posh, you really don't need a vast bank balance to put together a perfect outfit. In fact, it's never been easier to get the Knightsbridge look for next to nothing. I'm a big believer in saving up for special things, but I don't think there's any point splurging on head-to-toe designer labels for the sake of it. Also, you have to be much more creative to mix high end with high street. Lots of people have credit cards, but remember that you're the only one with your imagination.

Tearing up the wardrobe rule book

Ever since my mum told me I couldn't go to school dressed as a pirate, people have been telling me that there are all kinds of mysterious secret laws that are supposed to dictate the way we dress. Well, just like the screens of brand-new iPhones, rules are made to be broken. Over the last few years, I've been discovering that many of the things I've been told about fashion and clothes make no sense at all, so I've put together my own rules instead. Here are the thoughts that guide me when I'm thinking about what to wear.

Experts say: 'You can't go wrong with black.'
I say: 'Think pink!'
Of course, a few of us do look our best in black clothes. It's easy to wear black; you look pulled together and timeless. Most

> ❛I'm a big believer in saving up for special things, but I don't think there's any point splurging on head-to-toe designer labels for the sake of it.❜

importantly, black still looks classy, even if you're a serial spiller of red wine. However, I think that wearing all black, all day long can make me feel a bit down in the dumps. If you've got a meeting with your bank manager, or you're preparing to break up with someone, by all means be monochrome. But black simply isn't a staple that suits everyone, and there's no reason why all of our jeans and jumpers need to be black, just because the fashion police once said so. Maybe it dates back to the days when people were still scared of sabre-toothed tigers and felt the need to hide in the shadows at a moment's notice. Anyway, my favourite fashion staple is pink. A soft, peachy pink goes with absolutely everything. It's almost nude, which is neutral, and always seems soft and fresh – just what you should be wearing on those days when you get out of bed and need a hug. I think it's impossible not to smile when you wear pink, and if you bring a bit more of it into your life, you'll soon be grinning at your own reflection.

Experts say: 'You need one good pair of smart shoes.' I say: 'Get your heels from anywhere and splurge on trainers.'
Just the phrase 'smart shoes' makes me feel a bit tense, as though someone is going to chase me with an enormous can of hairspray,

all the way back to 1987. Even boys don't really bother with typical 'smart' shoes anymore, unless they were born in the 1940s or have to go to a funeral. Shoes have a major impact on your mood, so, if you're wearing something boring and functional on your feet, you're going to feel boring and functional all day. Occasionally, that's the vibe you're going for, but it shouldn't be your base state. If I'm honest, I have a few pairs of heels. OK, maybe a few hundred pairs. Still, I think this is just part of the human condition. High heels are meant to give us a brief burst of joy. Trainers make me feel *so good*. Especially when I'm putting them on after half an hour of stiletto wearing.

Other than my beloved Chanel pumps, which I save for the most special occasions, the footwear I get the most use out of is trainers. If I'm wearing heels, I'm trying to look smart for the office, where I'll be sitting down at a desk all day, or I'm going to a smart ball, and I'll kick them off as soon as it's time to get on the dance floor. If I'm going out for a proper night of dancing, or just nipping down the King's Road for essential supplies, only trainers can do the job. The nice thing is that there's so much choice now, and streetwear is super fashionable, so trainers can still be a glam, girly choice. Also, you can really see where your money goes, as most trainers have a technological element and are designed to protect your feet. If you like a bit of bling and have money to burn, you could splurge on something from Gucci's trainer range. If you just want something that will get you from A to B, blister free, something from Nike or Converse will absolutely do the job.

Experts say: 'Find your signature style.'
I say: 'Experiment like a mad scientist.'

Growing up, I remember some of my mum's friends had all sorts of strict rules about what did and didn't suit them. Some wouldn't be caught dead in horizontal stripes – literally, if they were run over on a zebra crossing, I think they'd crawl, bleeding, on to the pavement, in order to look better when the ambulance came. Some refused to wear black during the day, like vampires. Some feared short sleeves, to the point where they would rather pass out at a July barbecue than take their cardigans off. I think that fashion and style used to be much more rigid, and there was a real trend for telling women what they were not 'allowed' to do. There was this mad idea that you could only dress a certain way, depending on your body type, and, if you diverted from this, you might be sent to fashion jail, or at least forced to appear in court before Trinny and Susannah.

What's brilliant about fashion now is that it's for everyone, and we don't have to follow any ridiculous, made-up rules anymore. You can't be too old for a miniskirt, or not wear pink because you have red hair. I do think that, in time, we find that some looks suit us best, and we gravitate towards certain colours and shapes, but I also believe that we need to try *everything* before we figure out what looks best on us.

My only major 'rule' is that we need to get out of our comfort zone at least once a month. If you love looking really dressed up, spend a week in jeans and try to style them differently. If you wear a lot of monochrome, go mad and reach for something in bright yellow. If you've always got your legs out, see how you feel in a maxi. I think that it's really important to make sure you don't end up stuck in a style rut, and to keep being open to new ideas. It changes the way you see the world and makes you feel excited to be alive!

You don't have to spend a fortune on wardrobe updates, either. Keep an eye on eBay, and borrow your friends' clothes! You could even have a party where everyone has to bring the most bonkers item in their wardrobe, and you have to challenge each other to style it out.

Experts say: 'Get a sensible handbag.'
I say: 'Just be sensible about what you put in it.'

I mean, define sensible. Really. Our handbags are our hearts and our nervous systems. We cart our lives around in them and use them every day. You pick up your handbag just before you leave the house. How do you want to feel, in that moment? The right bag will make you feel like a bright, happy, capable, stylish, prepared person, but one that's too sensible will make you feel a bit dreary and battered. Again, there is a tendency to think that black and brown go with everything, but I think that handbags need to look interesting. This means that you can throw on anything you like, and a handbag will make you look stylish and put together.

Personally, I adore a clutch, and there are so many that come in cute colours. They're great for making an outfit look instantly coordinated. The trouble is that clutches are quite easy to lose. It's all very well, rushing out the door and thinking, *Well, all I need are my keys, bank card, phone and concealer,* only to come back eight hours later and realize you no longer have any of those essential life items. I'm not really sure what the solution is. Perhaps we need those special harnesses that mums put on their toddlers, to keep our clutches connected to us. Or bum bags. They're coming back in a big way. We can just pop the things we need in a bum bag, which is tied to our bodies and can't get lost, and then, if we lose the clutch, it doesn't matter, as it was just for decoration. Again, Gucci do some great bum bags, but you can just get one from ASOS if you've already spent all of your money on trainers.

One other useful thing you can do is use your handbags to store lip balms. If you're anything like me, you probably have at least forty lip balms in various states of fullness. If you put one in every bag you own, you'll never be caught out again!

Experts say: 'Dress your age.'
I say: 'Grab your granny's clothes.'

Don't laugh, but I have some outfits that my own granny probably wouldn't wear, because she'd think they were 'too old' for her. Stephanie Pratt once said to me, 'I don't know how you pull this off and still look young, and not like an old lady!' I think I love granny chic because you can be unapologetically feminine. It's a chance to be girly but grown-up at the same time. Also, I like to think that I'm just really well prepared. I'll have my granny look down, and when I'm an actual granny, I'll have it nailed – I'll just look slightly older!

Tweed is my favourite thing. It looks good with everything, at any time of day. A cropped tweed jacket with jeans and pumps is *very* Chelsea, but I'll wear the jacket with a little skirt and pearls for a date, or over a cute dress. For true granny chic, you need

> My friends have a tendency to plan parties with the strangest themes so I spend a lot of time standing in front of my wardrobe and wondering whether I've got anything that screams "Versailles" or "1960s Manhattan" or "Roaring Twenties Royalty".

masses of pearls, but, luckily, there are loads of modern, updated ones out there. Also, don't restrict yourself to necklaces. I love pearls as jacket buttons, hair pieces and even on shoes and bags.

The real secret to granny chic is to really embrace pastels. It helps to be a big fan of pink, but you can ease yourself in with cream and taupe while you're getting started. Honestly, it makes me look a lot more ladylike than I really am. I think that coordination is the key to that. Don't be afraid to make things match, and wearing shoes that go with your handbag will make you look as though you're permanently off to a power lunch, even if you're hungover and just about holding everything together with a combination of nerves and dry shampoo.

One thing that is vitally important is tights. Mark-Francis is the one who introduced me to the granny-chic look, and he says that runs and ladders are simply unacceptable. The trouble is, they're also inevitable, if you're the kind of person who is always twenty minutes late and running for a bus or scrambling out of a taxi. One thing always makes me feel professional and polished, and helps me seem much more together than I really am: spare tights. I keep a pair in my handbag, and some in my desk at the office. They're like a lucky charm and, as long as I'm prepared with a spare, I can usually make the tights that I'm actually wearing last a bit longer. This is partly because I don't want to have to go out and replace my spare pair. There is a very real danger that, when I die, my headstone will say, *Here lies Toff, who spent every single penny she earned on bloody tights.* I always have too many things to do, and not enough time to do them in as it is. I really, really don't want to spend many more hours of my life in a queue at Boots, clutching some emergency seventy deniers.

Looking the part: My most important outfits and what they mean to me

I think that what I love the most about dressing up is the way that certain clothes conjure up memories straight away. If I've had a really joyous night out, or if I was wearing something special because I was at a big work event, I can remember every single moment of the occasion by looking at a picture of what I was wearing. If I see something pink and ruffly, I instantly think about the beautiful Zeynep Kartal gown I wore to the National Television Awards, and the mix of excitement and dread I felt about having to

210

go and interview Dermot O'Leary. Whenever I'm wearing tweed, I remember the tweed jacket I wore for my interview at *The Lady*, and how I felt when I ripped the sleeve – and then what a lovely surprise it was to hear that I'd got the job! The thing that matters the most about what we wear is the way it makes us feel. So, here's a list of some of my favourite outfits of all time. I've picked them because I *felt* amazing in every single one.

The Black-and-White ball 2018 – Needle & Thread dress

There really is nothing I love more than a good full-length dress. It's even more fun to wear a maxi when it feels especially formal, and you know that everyone else will be getting their legs out – it makes you feel extra special. I was really panicking about what to wear to the Black-and-White ball. I'd been looking forward to it for ages, and, weirdly, that always makes it much harder to pick an outfit. Even though you know that what you wear doesn't matter that much, it matters to you. I think this was especially tricky because it was such a serious, grown-up occasion, and I'm sure that some of the stuffier guests expected me to turn up in a neon bikini. I spent hours lying awake, wondering what to do, before I asked for help. My brilliant P.A. came up with the solution, and it's one of the nicest dresses I've ever worn.

Ultimately, it couldn't be more me. It's a pale grey, demonstrating my well-documented love of pastel colours, in tiered lace, with shoestring straps and a ribbon sash. Technically, I think it might be a bridesmaid's dress, but there's no way I'd let my bridesmaids wear it if I was the one getting married – it's much too exciting!

That said, if any of my pals are getting hitched, I might see if they'll let me recycle it – at least that way I can save them some money!

It was especially important to get this right because my pal Stanley was my escort, and I didn't want his buddies to think he'd turned up with some flibbertigibbet. I needed to look more elegant than ever before. Even Boris said my dress was lovely! I tried to play it cool, but I was secretly screaming with joy on the inside. Of course, I returned the compliment the only way you can with Boris: I told him his hair looked smashing, too.

Long dresses are lovely because they have such a dramatic effect on the way you walk. They force you to hold yourself properly, and there's no chance of getting away with any slouching. That said, the other brilliant thing about them is that they really open up your footwear choices. You don't need to bother with heels if no one else can see them. I'm certain you could easily sneak some Air Force Ones under a formal gown and no one would be any the wiser.

The Jungle 2017 – red shorts and vest

Although we could choose what we wore during most of our time in the jungle, the red shorts became a kind of uniform, and I got totally into wearing them. It's funny, because I usually get quite upset when anyone tells me what to wear. When I was at school, I spent more effort and energy trying to subvert the uniform than I did revising for some of my exams. I think I could have got an A* in hair mussing, skirt rolling and advanced cuff scuffing. Still, maybe it's a sign of maturity, but I was really grateful for my smart red shorts. They really are my dream wardrobe item. Versatile, practical and sexy, but sensible. You can run around in them. You can wear them with a wide variety of tops, so they help you to get the most out of your other clothes – and they even have pockets.

I was also surprised to discover how much I liked the combination of long socks and boring brown boots. You do not want to get your legs out when you're surrounded by some of the world's most terrifying bugs and winged insects. I could dash through the undergrowth without worrying about scratches and scrapes.

Wearing a simple outfit helped me to focus on other things. It's impossible to put on a cream cashmere cardigan without constantly obsessing over what will happen if someone within a mile of you is holding a glass of red wine. My practical jungle clothes made me realize that there is a middle ground between dressing up to within an inch of your life and dressing down to a point that frightens the pizza-delivery person. Also, I've said it before, but I'll say it again: those pockets were a revelation. I loved them so much that, when I left the jungle, I was almost cured of my handbag addiction. (Of course, I'm back on the bags now.)

Cannes 2018 – bikini and heels

Some people make a very big deal out of eating seasonally. They only have tomatoes in the summer, sprouts at Christmas, and they would never dream of touching asparagus after the clocks had gone back, presumably because they're scared that someone from the River Cafe would start banging on their windows with a broom handle if they so much as considered it. I'm a bit more

213

chilled out – I mean, Nando's is always in season, surely? Yet, it's very important to me to dress in a way that reflects my natural surroundings. So, if I'm skiing, ideally I'd like some Fendi snow boots to change into afterwards. If I'm dancing, I need sequins. And, if I'm on a yacht, I have to wear a bikini and heels. It's the only outfit that makes any sense in that climate.

If you're outside in the South of France at any point between June and September, you *must* wear a bikini or you'll be vaporized by the heat. And heels might seem a bit silly, but they do help if someone has invited you to hang out on their yacht. You'll look prepared.

When I filmed the *Made in Chelsea* summer special in 2016, I coordinated every bikini I brought with a pair of heels, and I felt like a Bond girl for about twenty seconds every day, before I got bored of posing around the pool and flopped on to a sun lounger. Still, I felt very pleased with myself, and most importantly of all, I spent quite a lot of the trip hanging out on yachts! I learned something very useful that summer: a stiletto heel looks amazing, but if you're by a pool or on the beach, you're even more likely than usual to fall on your arse. A wedge espadrille does everything that you want a heel to do, but it also allows you to walk around without stacking it and spilling your drink. A true multitasker.

The Oscars 2018 – Alessandra Rich maxi

What do you wear when you're thousands of miles from home, excited, nervous and about to do one of the most important jobs of your career? Especially when you know that more people than ever before will be taking your photograph and judging your choice of outfit? You need to feel as confident as possible, but you need to know that everyone will love your look as much as you do.

Incidentally, I think this is one of the most difficult things about our societal social-media saturation point. Now, you *know* I love Insta nearly as much as I love my mum, but it does make event dressing tricky, because you feel obliged to wear something new every time you go out. If you recycle, it looks like a statement. If you're dressing up for a big night, it really piles the pressure on – as if there wasn't loads of pressure already.

I knew that the Oscars was a once-in-a-lifetime occasion, and I needed a once-in-a-lifetime dress, so I rented one. This is actually a brilliant idea, because it opens up a brand-new wardrobe of beautiful things to borrow, and you can have a night of fun before giving them back. It's much better than constantly feeling slightly guilty every time you open your wardrobe and see an incredibly expensive dress shaming you for only wearing it once. Also, I've noticed that you're much more careful when you've paid a hefty security deposit than you are when you borrow something from a friend. Renting generally leads to much better inter-pal relations, and far fewer cigarette burns. Still, I wasn't entirely immune to disaster. When we finished the live item, I raised my arms in the air and cheered, because I hadn't slept for a week and I was *quite* excited about the prospect of going to bed. To my horror, I broke the arm of the dress and my amazing P.A. had to sew me back in! Still, it could have been worse. At least it didn't happen live on air.

Anyway, this Alessandra Rich dress is one of the most stunning things I have ever worn. It was cream, silk and made me feel like a Greek goddess. There was even a high leg-slit, so I could do my best Angelina Jolie impression when I was near the red carpet. While I love fashion and shopping, at twenty-three I'm still finding looks I love and working out exactly who I am, style-wise. If you feel as though you're in a bit of a rut, and you're bored of your clothes, but you're nervous about going for a serious splurge, I definitely recommend renting something. It gives you the chance to rifle through a gorgeous, glamorous, grown-up dressing-up box.

Sunday Times Style *magazine cover – Pink Burberry coat*

Choosing my outfit for the cover of *Style* magazine was a little bit daunting. To be honest, I was hoping they would let me go for something that looked seriously grown-up, and maybe slightly strict and severe. I was hoping for a dash of tweed, a pussy-bow blouse and maybe some tortoiseshell spectacles. I wasn't expecting to look like a big pink teddy bear! That Burberry fur was a coat of dreams. The second I put it on, I had a 'pinch me' moment. I looked in the mirror and thought, *Is that really me? Am I wearing this divine coat on the cover of* Style? It was a real dream come true.

It's my very favourite shade of pink, and I love looking soft and cosy. I like to think that the picture captured the fun side of me, and, if I'd gone for tweed and specs, I might have ended up scaring a few readers away.

It's so important to be open and collaborative, and I'm so lucky to work with stylists who give me the chance to wear clothes I'd never have picked for myself. The trouble is that you usually have to give it back at the end of the shoot, when you've fallen in love with it!

My five make-up must-haves

As you know, on an ideal day, I put my concealer on before I brush my teeth. Make-up makes me feel as though I'm ready to face the world, and while I'm getting more comfortable with my bare face, I simply feel much more like me when I'm armed with a fully packed make-up bag and I'm able to take control of the way I look. Here are my cosmetic essentials – and I'm pretty sure they would enhance anyone's make-up bag.

Estée Lauder Double Wear concealer and foundation

After trying every single concealer there is, I've decided that Double Wear is my all-time favourite. It's basically Tippex for the face. If you've just got a tattoo and you don't want your mum to know about it, simply cover it in Double Wear and she'll be none the wiser. It's also perfect for when you've got a big event coming up, there's a job interview on the horizon, or you're getting married in the morning. You know how sometimes your skin turns psychic and decides to look extra bad when you need it to look better than ever? I'm sure that it can sense when Double Wear is on the premises, and it's forced to behave itself.

Hourglass Vanish Flash highlighter

This is heaven in a tube. Instant cheekbones for everyone, and it's shaped like a Toblerone. Plus, it looks incredibly glam at night, but it's simply deliciously dewy in the day. I'm in love with it.

Elizabeth Arden Eight Hour cream

This is the one that your mum raved about, and you thought she was being a bit boring. Well, your mum and mine were on to something. It can heal any cut, scrape or chapped lip, it works as hand cream, and, if you're feeling adventurous, you can even put some on your eyelids and make them gleam. (It also keeps your eyebrows in place. So clever!)

Any pink lipstick

I mean, you can't go wrong with YSL or Chanel, but every single handbag I own has about five different brands of pinky-nude lippy rolling around in the bottom. I adore a pale pink because I do favour the sweet and girly, but, more importantly, if you're a wine-loving chatterbox, as I am, a pale shade doesn't need as much retouching as a bright red lippy.

Essie Ballet Slippers nail polish

This has been one of my favourite shades ever since I found out that the Queen wears it! It goes with absolutely everything and, again, it's not too high maintenance. If you smudge it a bit because you're too impatient to let it dry properly (ahem), no one really notices.

My Skin

We've all had spots at some point in our lives. I think that every single one of us has woken up in the morning, felt a tingle around the chin and worried that our day might be ruined. There is no such thing as perfect skin, and no one has a clear complexion all the time. So, it's strange that we only ever see people in the public eye who look flawless and poreless. You never see anyone on T.V. struggling with a breakout. Well, almost never. Which is why I eventually decided it was really important for me to get in front of the camera, make-up free.

I need to backtrack a little bit. I started struggling with my skin just before I turned twenty. For almost all of my teens, I had a clear complexion, and I totally took it for granted. The trouble began in the autumn, when I'd just started working on *Made in Chelsea* and I'd come back to university. At first, I had a couple of painful spots on my chin and jawline. They hurt, but more than anything, they annoyed me. I tried the usual tricks – slathering them in concealer by day, and toothpaste at night – but matters did not improve.

I assumed I was simply stressed, and that things would clear up if I tried to have some early nights and swapped wine for water – which is probably what Jesus would have done, if there were more passages in the Bible about skincare. The toothpaste simply burned through my skin and the spots got worse. (If you're reading for beauty tips, here is the best advice I can possibly give you: never, ever put toothpaste on your skin. It's an urban myth. It doesn't dry out your spots, it just makes the rest of your skin red and causes it to peel. Slather your spots in Colgate at night and you'll wake up to more misery and a minty fresh pillow. You might as well put chewing gum in your hair – it would cause slightly less damage.)

Uncomfortable in my own skin

It wasn't a great time to start my T.V. career. I'd never been more self-conscious about the way my face looked, and there was a camera pointing at it constantly. I loved the work, and I knew that being on the show was the opportunity of a lifetime, but uni stress was making me anxious and miserable, and my skin got worse.

I went to an introductory session for my politics course, where all of the students had to introduce themselves to the rest of the group. When it was my turn, I took a deep breath and smiled.

'My name's Georgia, I studied English, History and Economics, and I'm really excited about studying Politics, which is one of my greatest passions.'

A voice at the back of the room interrupted me: 'You forgot to say you're a *Made in Chelsea* ****,' they yelled.

I looked at my tutor and waited for them to discipline the boy who had just called me one of the worst words in the English language while we were all in a classroom together. Nothing happened. I bit my lip and tried not to burst into tears. I felt flushed with shame and embarrassment, and my burning cheeks made my growing collection of spots seem even more painful. I knew that everyone was staring at me.

If my skin had been clear, I would have felt much more confident. I could have met his gaze, raised my eyebrows and stared him down, but, in the moment, I felt awkward, ugly and alone. It was a horribly vicious circle. Being at university, and juggling my studies with a demanding job, made me extremely stressed and anxious. The stress was making my skin worse, which made my anxiety worse – and so my skin kept deteriorating. Outside uni, I was having the time of my life, but thoughts of studying and spots were constantly lurking in the back of my brain and making me sad and worried. At least I could try to ignore the bad feelings that my uni course was causing, but the spots were unavoidable. They were the first thing I saw in the mirror every morning.

Asking for help

Eventually, I decided to take charge of the situation. I spoke to a life coach, who helped me to see that I loved everything about my life apart from my degree course. This is when I quit uni to become a nanny. Leaving university didn't fix my acne, but it definitely made it slightly less ferocious and more manageable. My spots weren't so bad, but the stress of the previous months had left me with significant scarring. I was worried about the way it looked, but also, it was very painful. Even if my skin was relatively calm, my face always felt sore. I couldn't ignore the fact that it was difficult to be filmed so frequently and to constantly worry about how my face would look on screen. I'd dread Monday nights when fans would watch the show and tweet about it. I lived in fear that someone on social media would say something mean about my acne. So, I went to get some medical help.

Going to see a doctor about my skin was even more nerve wracking than going to the life coach. It meant having to be out in public without wearing any make-up and showing a stranger the state of my bare face. One of the hardest parts was probably the fact that I had to be honest about the problem. I couldn't ignore it, or pretend it wasn't bothering me. My skin was so bad that, for a long time, I was embarrassed to seek help. I still can't speak about my skin without crying, because it makes me feel so vulnerable. I was genuinely worried the doctor would say, 'You've got the worst skin I've seen in all my years of practising medicine!' Obviously, this did not happen! They were kind and compassionate and they didn't judge me. I was prescribed Roaccutane, which is a heavy-duty drug. It works by slowing down the amount of oil that your skin releases, but the side effects can be extreme, which is why most doctors only prescribe it in severe cases.

For a while, the Roaccutane really seemed to be making a difference, but my doctor said I had to stop taking it during the summer of 2016, when I was filming *Made in Chelsea* in the South of France. The chemical it contains, isotretinoin, makes your skin extremely sensitive to sunlight, and you have to avoid direct sun exposure if you're taking it. I had two options: spend the whole summer indoors, wrapped in hats and blankets, or come off the medication and hope that my skin stayed OK.

Summer of fun

So, I went to Cannes, dressed as a bee keeper and locked myself in my room . . . *Obviously*, I'm kidding. I crossed my fingers and toes and left my pills at home, and ended up having one of the most brilliant summers of my life. Everything worked out perfectly. I was sharing a villa with my BFFs Ollie and Binky, and I don't think I've ever been happier. Every single day was hilarious. At the time, we were all single, and talked about boys *constantly*. (By the following summer, Binky had got back together with her boyfriend, JP, and she was pregnant, so I think that we all feel quite nostalgic when we think about that summer – it was a time when none of us were proper grown-ups.)

Even though it was really hot, Binky kept making a fat-burning pea and ham hock soup. I think the idea was that it was a protein-heavy, filling dinner that would stop us from stuffing our faces with ice cream – but it just made us fart. There were days when the three of us would sit around, farting *constantly*. Of course, we couldn't stop laughing – and the more we laughed, the worse it got! I suspect that everyone else was relieved they didn't have to share with us and our farts.

Every night, I'd go out in the little Fiat Panda that I'd hired. (Ollie and Binky found this hilarious, but I was too young to be insured on anything else!) I'd go to a seriously sketchy car park, outside Cannes, not knowing whether the car would still be there when I came back – I reckon that it would have been nicked if it was a slightly more exciting model – and I'd go off and have ridiculous adventures. Once, I met some fab new friends who asked me if I wanted to come on board their boat. Of *course* I did! However, I was still there the next morning when I got a panicked phone call from Ollie, wondering where I was and why I hadn't come home.

'Look on Google Maps and call me back – I'll come and get you!' he promised.

I checked and phoned him. 'Um . . . It says I'm in the sea.'

Being with my best friends and feeling totally relaxed and happy meant that my skin stayed fairly clear, even on a diet of cocktails, late nights and no medication. (Maybe Binky's fart soup had secret skin-boosting properties, too . . .) Even my failed romance with Francis Boulle didn't bother me. I felt as though my confidence was at an all-time high, because I'd stopped thinking about my skin. So, when I came back, I asked my agent Matt to think about suggesting me for the 2017 series of *I'm A Celebrity . . . Get Me Out Of Here!* I'd had such a great time in France that I longed for another jolly, and I thought it looked like such fun. This is the magic of confidence. It makes you think, *Well, nothing ventured, nothing gained.* I didn't think I'd get the job, but, at the time, I felt as though I had nothing to lose. Nearly a year later, after several interviews and nail-biting moments, I'd gone from thinking, *If it happens, it happens,* to, *I am so desperate to go to Australia that I will send the producers a video of me eating a wasps' nest to show how committed I am.* I got the call. I was off to the jungle!

Bare-faced in the jungle

However, my old problem was back. My skin was worse than ever, and I couldn't take my medication with me, because of the risk of sun exposure. I'd gone back on the Roaccutane especially, to get ready for the jungle, and sometimes it makes your spots much worse before it makes them better. We'd be exposed, warts and all. Or, in my case, spots and all. I decided that it might be OK, if I was allowed to bring concealer as my luxury item, but I was still desperately anxious. I flew out on my own, and struggled to read my book, concentrate on any of the in-flight films, or even take full advantage of the drinks trolley! I couldn't stop thinking about my skin, even with the help of a stiff gin and tonic, and Will Ferrell at his funniest.

Then, just after I arrived in Australia, I had some terrible news. I was talking to one of the producers about how worried I was about my spots, but trying to make the best of it. Already, I'd broken the rules a bit by pouring three bottles of Double Wear into the same pot, so it counted as one item. 'As long as I can put it on first thing, I'll be fine!' I smiled.

It made a huge difference for me. Ironically, I feel like my most authentic version of myself when I've got my concealer on. If I'd gone into the jungle without it, I would have been shy, grumpy and awkward. I might not have been able to talk to anyone. The first few days would have been completely different. As it was, the more fun I had, and the better my friendships became, the more comfortable I felt. I'm most proud of the day that I brushed my teeth before putting my concealer on first. Surviving the challenges and building brand-new relationships meant that, for the first time since my teens, I truly felt confident in my own skin.

The big reveal

For *This Morning*, I interviewed the consultant dermatologist Dr Anjali Mahto, and she told me that lots of people don't seek help because they think acne is a 'cosmetic issue', and that there's nothing serious about spots – but it's actually a significant medical problem. Dr Mahto told me that people who suffer with acne are much more likely to have depression. This is why it's so important for me to speak out about it. There's so much that we still don't understand about how to treat it, but I know that, if I talk about my experiences, hopefully people won't suffer in silence as I did.

I knew that I had a serious medical problem with my skin, but it was difficult to make people understand how I truly felt about it, possibly because I wasn't being com-

> **" I know how it feels to wake up on a really bad day and feel so self-conscious about my spots that I can't leave the house. "**

pletely honest with myself. Going into the jungle made me realize that this wasn't just about me being a bit girly and missing my make-up. It showed me that it was OK to have an emotional relationship with my skin, and that I wasn't alone. Plenty of other people were struggling in silence, too.

When my mum flew out to see me, the first thing she said to me when she hugged me was, 'I'm so proud of you. You're really helping people.' I had no idea what she was talking about until she explained that people had been getting in touch on social media to say that they loved seeing my skin, and it meant a lot to them because they also struggled with their complexions. To be honest, I thought that I was being brave by eating things, climbing up things and not freaking out about things that might be poisonous, but it turned out that the biggest, best thing I did was bearing my face. That's what inspired people.

Of course, life is never quite as straightforward as we'd like it to be, and, for every lovely comment or message someone sent about the difference I was making, I'd get a cruel troll calling me 'pizza face', talking about the 'craters' in my complexion, or worse. I just don't know what motivates someone to make that sort of comment. Do they think they're helping? Are they under the impression that their acid tongues will somehow dry out the spots and make my skin clear?

I don't think these people realize just how hurtful these comments are. Firstly, it's easy for them to think that I won't read them. I'm on T.V., they will never meet me, and it probably seems as though they're just bitching into a void. It's cowardly, and I don't think they would ever say anything so unkind to my face, but it still hurts me and makes me sad. Secondly, there may well be people in their lives who really struggle with their skin. If these people know what their friends and family are saying about my complexion, they won't be able to go to them for help and support. I've always tried hard to be positive and kind, but dealing with trolls has made me extra determined to never bitch about the way someone else looks. It's also made me committed to being open about my skin struggles, instead of trying to hide away. When we pretend to be perfect, no one wins. But even though going without make-up is incredibly hard for me, I know it's worth it when it helps someone else.

To be completely honest with you, I've found it incredibly difficult to get to this point. When *This Morning* first phoned and said they wanted me to film a skincare segment where I went without make-up, I told them I couldn't do it. At the time, I was on a real high. I'd just got back from the jungle, I was doing more presenting work and I felt so excited about my career and my future. Showing my spots seemed so scary, and I was worried that I'd lose all of the confidence I'd worked so hard to build up. Reporting from the red carpet at the Oscars was a piece of cake. Styling out a mistake I'd made on live T.V., or rehearsing changes during a broadcast, with ten minutes until I went on camera? Absolutely! No worries! I could take it all in my stride. But the idea of taking my make-up off in front of people gave me chills. I kept coming up with excuses. But the more I put it off, the more messages I received from people who felt just as bad about their own skin as I felt about mine. If I couldn't be brave on my own, I had to make myself do it for them.

I will never forget the way it felt to sit on the bed in Dr Mahto's office, knowing I was on camera and I was about to drop my mask. The moment that she started cleaning off my make-up with a tissue made my stomach sink. It was a bit like going on a really terrifying rollercoaster, telling yourself that it will definitely be OK, then catching sight of the first big loop just as the bar comes down, and wanting to scream, 'No! Sorry! I've changed my mind! Please, let me off!' But I will never regret doing it. I got so much lovely feedback, and so many positive comments from other people who have been suffering, too. Even though I know that I'm incredibly fortunate in thousands of ways, I know how it feels to wake up on a really bad day and feel so self-conscious about my spots that I can't leave the house. However, it's so much easier when you know that you're not alone.

Learning to accept my imperfections

I hope I've helped all of the people who have reached out to me, but they've helped me, too. It's very difficult to stop worrying about the fact that people might be staring at you while judging and commenting. Taking my make-up off on *This Morning* means that I never need to worry about being caught out, because everyone has already seen me in my most raw, vulnerable state. I don't care whether I fall down the escalator in Harvey Nicks, or accidentally trip up in Loulou's and spill red wine all over Prince Harry. Nothing can embarrass me now!

In all seriousness, it isn't just our skin that makes us self-conscious, and if this journey has taught me anything, it's that we're all constantly worried about who's looking at us and what they're thinking, even though most people aren't looking at all. They're obsessing about their own flaws and insecurities, and praying that you won't notice them. One of the best things I've done for my skin is taking it seriously, seeking medical advice and getting treatment. The other is that I've stopped seeing my skin as a flaw. It's not an embarrassing secret that I have to hide from everyone. It's a part of who I am, just like my laugh, my enthusiasm and my Deliveroo addiction. (OK, that last one possibly *is* a flaw.) I would love to have a clear complexion, but

I'm starting to realize my spots themselves aren't the problem. The issue is that I've spent months of my life focusing on them, investing huge amounts of energy into dwelling on something negative that makes me feel so sad. A positive attitude is much harder to cultivate than a skincare routine, but it does us so much good in the long run.

Accepting our imperfections isn't the same as deciding that we're perfect. It's about realizing that perfection is an unattainable state and trying to like ourselves as we are. It's scarily easy to let our vulnerabilities rule our lives, but it's important to keep some perspective on them. After I was on *This Morning*, hardly anyone wanted to talk about the state of my skin. Everyone was much more interested in the fact that I overcame a personal challenge by showing it on camera. Most importantly, I learned and grew from the experience. I hope that I look back to my work with Dr Mahto and see how I grew as a journalist and presenter. It's given me the confidence to take on bigger work challenges and, also, not to be afraid of putting my personality into my work. Filming my trip to the surgery was the most serious thing that I'd ever done at that point. Although I was really proud of my presenting, the focus had always been on fun. This experience showed me that I was capable of tackling heavier topics – and that people wanted to hear what I had to say, even if I wasn't making them laugh.

If you don't have any issues with your skin, there might be something else in your life that scares you, and you might spend a lot of time trying to hide your feelings about it and trying to stop people from finding out. If you were to face your fears, you'd probably realize that everything is much more dramatic and terrifying when it stays in your head. If you're honest with yourself about the way you feel, and you ask for help, you'll be in a position to deal with the problem. Even more importantly, you'll be able to pursue positive, exciting opportunities, because you won't be secretly obsessing about your fears and flaws.

The greatest lesson I've learned is that everyone has an insecurity that holds them back. The trolls who say cruel things only do so because they're scared, too, and they're worried about being found out. No one expects you to be perfect – they're too busy worrying about the fact that their own imperfections are going to be exposed. Life is so much more fun and fulfilling when you can see your flaws and insecurities in the context of who you are as a person. There's always more good than bad, and the best way to banish the bad is to concentrate on the good.

> ❛ I'd dread Monday nights when Made in Chelsea aired and fans would tweet about it. I lived in fear that someone on social media would say something mean about my acne. ❜

Toff's top skincare dos and don'ts

My skincare journey has been an emotional one, but obviously I've found lots of great practical hints and tips, too. These are my favourites, and the ones that have worked best for me. If you've struggled with your skin, I hope they help!

Do take your skin seriously

One of my biggest regrets is that it took me such a long time to do anything about my skin, because I thought it might just clear up and go away. I tried giving up alcohol, wheat and dairy before I got medical advice. For some people, this really works, but promise me that you'll chat to a doctor before you think about giving up cheese forever.

Don't take unsolicited advice

Because of my job, I'm in a position where trolls can tweet me and say the most *horrible* things about my skin. But at least I don't have to worry about what they might be thinking, because they've made it very clear! Before I went to the jungle, my biggest problem was the kind, well meaning, but *incredibly* irritating people who would tell me how to sort out my spots, in the middle of a nice chat about holidays or pubs or west London traffic jams. 'You've got spots! I know what helps spots!' they would say, sometimes prodding my painful face and adding their germs to my collection. Firstly, it made me feel so embarrassed, as though they had been thinking about the state of my face for our whole conversation.

Secondly, did they really think they were giving me new information? I *had* spots, and I was trying everything! I lost count of the people who told me to put toothpaste on them, long after my own personal Colgate-gate. Now I say, 'Oh? Are you a qualified dermatologist? I always thought you were a quantity surveyor/ interior decorator/dog walker?' That will shut them up.

Do keep your toothpaste far from your face

Yes, I know I'm not giving you any new information, but I honestly can't stress it enough. Don't put it anywhere but on a brush, inside your mouth.

Don't go straight for the drugs

They are incredibly helpful for lots of people, including me, but they're strong and serious. Your doctor might suggest all kinds of alternatives. Some people use steroid cream, and others find that going on the pill really helps their skin. It might even be an allergy to something in your cleanser or moisturizer, which means you can fix it by switching brands. Prescription medication can make a huge difference, but it doesn't necessarily mean it's for you. We're all different.

Do wear as much concealer as you like

It's your face, and the way you present it to the world is up to you, and absolutely no one else. If you feel brave and confident about not wearing make-up in public, that's brilliant. Equally, if you feel like your best and bravest self under four layers of foundation, that's fine too. The way you feel is all that matters, and other people's opinions aren't worth thinking about. However, do check the ingredients of your concealer and make sure that there isn't anything in it that might be aggravating your skin. There's a range of medicated concealers available that can help milder acne, but do some research and find out what will work best for you. Some people find that it's best to use oil-free make-up, but others find that some oils, like tea tree and thyme, bring their acne inflammation down. Again, it's an individual choice. Remember that we're all different!

Don't pick your spots!

This is some of the oldest advice in the world, and it can be the hardest to follow. If your spots are painful, it's extremely tempting to pick, squeeze and rub. I promise that it's always best to leave them alone. If it's really difficult, try to work out a rewards system. A new lipstick if you can go without touching your spots for a week, or a night out if you can manage a month. To be honest, this works for anything that's hard, like not texting a terrible ex, or exam revision. If doing the right thing is difficult, give yourself some incentives.

Do focus on the positives

When my skin was at its worst, I found that it helped to make the most of the parts of my appearance that I really like. I would stick on an extra coat of mascara, or make a big effort with my hair, just to remind myself that feeling good about my face and body doesn't mean hiding it altogether. It's important to find something about the way you look that's worth celebrating.

Don't feel bad about feeling sad

Hopefully, there will come a point when you feel able to accept your skin as a part of who you are, and it doesn't dominate your thoughts. However, as Dr Mahto told me, skin conditions can have a significant impact on our mental health. It's OK to have those days where you simply give in to the fact that you feel low, and you can't find anything good about what you see in the mirror. What's important is that you talk to your friends and family about the way you're feeling and remember that you won't feel this way forever. It *will* get better, and brighter days are right around the corner.

Positivity

I'm a great believer in drains and radiators. Not just for the purposes of sanitation and central heating, although those are some of my favourite aspects of being alive in the twenty-first century, instead of being born in, say, medieval England. But, when it comes down to it, we're all Drains or Radiators.

Sadly, we all know a Drain or two. These are the people who you go out for a drink with and then come home feeling mysteriously morose, decidedly down in the dumps, and you wonder whether you're on the brink of a particularly bad flu. It can take a little while to identify a Drain, but the way you feel after you've spent time with them is the biggest and most reliable clue. We all have wobbly moments and difficult periods where we need to have a little whinge to our best friends, but Drains do nothing but whinge. Their glass isn't just half empty, there's a cigarette butt and a drowned fly floating in it. (The fly possibly dived in after hearing the Drain complain, deciding that its life really wasn't worth living.)

A Drain could win the lottery and their first thought would be a miserable one about tax. Ask a Drain about their last holiday and you'll hear a miserable tale of sunstroke, stolen sun loungers and flights filled with crying babies. Drains are unlucky in love, and when I say unlucky, I mean that it doesn't matter how ravishingly beautiful or well-endowed they are, they're so tedious that new lovers would rather do a bunk through the window of the downstairs loo than listen to another second of self-pity.

This is why I've always tried to be a Radiator. My favourite friends are Radiators, and they set such a lovely, glowing example of shiny joy that they turn everyone else around them into Radiators, too. A cup of tea with a Radiator will make you feel as though you've spent an afternoon at a spa, enjoying a full-body massage, and then been fed a bowl of Ready Brek. If a Radiator is burgled, they'll laugh it off – and celebrate, if the burglar took the hideous picture their aunt painted on a course in Tuscany, but left the gin.

Radiators are generous and, when your life is going well, they'll celebrate your successes. If you get a promotion, they'll be on your doorstep with a bottle of champagne, and they'll never point out the fact that your new job comes with a raise of just 10p an hour and you need to be at the office at six in the morning. (But it won't! We'll come to the art of negotiating, later in the book!) Anyway, if you can find a way to cultivate your inner Radiator, you'll win friends, influence people, and never go short of a party invitation ever again.

I've always been a very positive person, and I've been told that I'm one of nature's Radiators. Of course, my life isn't perfect, and sometimes big and little things get me down, but I always do my best to bounce back quickly. Sometimes, I think I'm like a puppy. If I'm sad for a second, it doesn't take me long to find something to be excited about. If there's a secret to it, I think that's probably it.

> **There is always something in life to look forward to, even if it's just lunch.**

Life can be hard and horrible, but it can also be brilliant and amazing, and if you can find the fun and joy in small things, you will radiate, and the big things will come your way. I mean, unlike most puppies, we might not be distracted from our troubles by having someone chuck a ball into the Serpentine, but there's always dinner! That's never not exciting!

I've made a list of positivity tips for when life is feeling less than lovely. This is what I do when I really need a boost. Whether I'm trying to fight the ultimate forces of evil, Internet trolls, or I've just lost another set of house keys, these are the things I do to cheer myself up. They work!

Try some time travel

Surely, actual time travel will be possible any day now. I mean, if 3-D printers are a thing, why not time machines? Firstly, I'd go back to the Roaring Twenties, party with Fitzgerald and Hemingway, and find some fabulous barman to give me the ultimate cocktail-making course. Then I would return to the twenty-first century, to just a couple of years ago, confront my terrible ex and say, 'You have not behaved like a gentleman, and I'm a true lady, so we were never going to be compatible,' instead of bursting into tears and screaming, 'I hate you – you're a bellend!'

Anyway, we might not have full, thrilling access to Tardis-style time travel just yet, but we can visit the past and the future in our minds. If I'm having an awful day, I try to remember how I coped with adversity in the past, and how it's affecting me right now. I still remember crying after my teacher told me off in class for talking – which was fair; I was a persistent offender. But that afternoon is a distant memory, and although my chatty tendencies might not have done me any favours in the classroom, I've built a career on them. Quite often, when something makes you sad, you feel as though the world is ending. Yet, a week or a month later, either everything worked out for the best, or you can't even remember what it was that upset you so much. You've always got the power to recover from a disaster, you just need to remind yourself of the times you've done it before, and you'll do it again.

Get moving

Don't laugh, but I love exercise, even though I've always been slightly suspicious of people who take it extremely seriously. Lots of people are keen to make us feel as though we need to be earnest, even humourless, to embrace fitness. However, I've just discovered the opposite is true. Sport can be silly. Running up and down the pavement like a mad thing is sometimes the greatest cure for everything from heartache to overdraft blues. If you're struggling to feel positive, it's because your head is concentrating on a difficult situation. When you do something with your body, your brain can't focus on the bad. You don't need to go to a special class or buy any equipment. You can even manage without trainers. Sometimes, I just put on some nineties pop and throw myself around the room. Star jumps and the Spice Girls are my favourite combination. You boost your circulation, your endorphins flow and you're bound to feel more cheerful.

If you're committed to being a Radiator, and I hope you are, you might want to find a class you love, or make sport a regular part of your schedule. My favourite part of Games at school was always being a member of a team. When you have to work together, listen, watch and communicate, you have to concentrate, which means that you don't have time to worry, or feel stressed and self-conscious. Even if you didn't enjoy netball at school, you might discover that you love it as a grown-up. Especially because there's no shouty games-mistress trying to stop pupils sloping off for a smoke at the bottom of the field.

Curate a box of joy

When we do almost everything online, physical things like cards, notes and photos become extra special. One great way to cheer yourself up is to buy a beautiful box – it doesn't need to be expensive, just really pretty – and fill it up with anything you've kept that has a great memory attached. Fill it with cinema tickets, boarding passes, shells from the beach, cards from flowers – and it's especially important to include any cards or mementoes you have congratulating you for things you've achieved. Once you've organized your box, you can keep adding to it, and then open it whenever you need a burst of joy, positivity and confidence. One thing I will warn against is including mementoes from exes. No matter how lovely the memory is, this might backfire. On the other hand, there is nothing to stop you from making your own cards and notes, and putting them in the box. So, instead of hanging on to the packet of Love Hearts your very first boyfriend gave you on Valentine's Day, write yourself a message congratulating yourself for not calling your ex for a week.

Go natural

There is a reason why everyone I know who lives in Chelsea is constantly going on about how good it feels to get out of London. The city is my home, and I love it dearly, but, sometimes, no shop, bar or restaurant can be quite as calming and restorative as looking at some deer grazing under a big tree. I suspect most Drains are drained by the demands of modern life, and it's much harder to become a Drain if you spend a lot of time outside, where there are no Wi-Fi passwords. I grew up beside the sea, and being close to the ocean is a wonderful way to feel rested and shake off some stress. Some research has found that spending time outside in nature makes our brains quicker and more creative, so if a problem is making you sad, you're bound to find a solution if you head for the great outdoors and get some fresh air.

Activate 'The Vault'

Most of the time, the best way to feel positive is to focus on some seriously good things – but, sometimes, the only way to get past any negative feelings is to power through them. The path to positivity is occasionally filled with muddy puddles. If I'm in a seriously bad mood, and nothing can shake it, I call one of my closest friends and tell them that I need to make a deposit in The Vault. This doesn't mean going to a spooky old bank, or the lair of a Mr Burns style baddie; it's telling your darkest, saddest secrets to someone you trust with all your heart, before they promise to lock them away forever. Telling your troubles to a sympathetic listener is a great way to clear your head, and sometimes saying what's bothering you out loud is enough to make you realize that nothing is as bad as it seems. One word of warning about The Vault is that it only really works if you speak to someone. Writing an enormous email doesn't do the job, and there's always a risk that those words might come back to haunt you. Also, you have to be absolutely sure of the person you're telling. Don't risk confiding in someone who might sneak!

Try tanning!

We all know that the sun cheers us up when we're feeling blue, but the sun doesn't shine every day – not even in Chelsea, where everything seems to have a golden glow and the rain looks like it's fallen through the Nashville filter on its way down from the sky.

However, you can buy bottles of sunshine from Boots, and they're almost as good as a trip to the Caribbean. If both body and soul feel wintry, I know it's time to get the fake tan out. An afternoon of bronzing can banish the most persistent of blues. Take your time over your tan. Exfoliate properly, apply carefully, and don't go anywhere near any cream carpets, because nothing will kill your vibe like a big brown stain in the middle of the floor. I've made some bad life decisions in my time, but the worst have involved me being naked, slightly sticky and hunting for the bleach.

Tomorrow might be amazing

When you're feeling sad, scared and worried about the way the world is, and your place in it, it's normal to obsess about the worst-case scenarios. We look for the negative, assume the worst, and then wonder whether we're jinxing ourselves. If I go to sleep thinking, *I hope I don't get a spot,* then you can guess what will happen when I get up the next morning! Of course, something bad might happen, and it's natural for us to worry and wonder how we can protect our present selves from our future ones. But, equally, tomorrow might be brilliant! There is always something in life to look forward to, even if it's just lunch. Something terrible might happen tomorrow, but something unexpectedly amazing might happen, too. If everything is horrible right now, at least you're getting it out of the way and improving the odds for fun and fabulousness. When you look for positive signs, you see them everywhere.

Ten songs to put a smile on your face:

'You Make My Dreams' by Daryl Hall & John Oates

♫

'Life is a Rollercoaster' by Ronan Keating

♫

'Beautiful' by Snoop Dogg

♫

'Safe and Sound' by Capital Cities

♫

'Dancing Queen' by Abba

♫

'Chocolate' by 1975

♫

'Dog Days Are Over' by Florence + the Machine

♫

'Golden' by Jill Scott

♫

'9 to 5' by Dolly Parton

♫

'Loving is Easy' by Rex Orange County

Mentors

I know there's a certain amount of luck involved in meeting people who inspire you and who you can learn from, and I feel so, so fortunate to have so many incredible people in my life. I still can't quite believe that, not only has Stanley given me advice, he's in my phone book! However, I do think there's an element of making your own luck. The wise, stimulating, motivating people aren't standing in the street wearing sandwich boards that say, *Ask me for life hacks!* You have to look for them and be open to the fact that the help and support they can offer you might not be offered in a straightforward way. As soon as you train yourself to look for mentors, you'll be spotting them everywhere! Here's how to get started.

Always keep listening

This is such an obvious tip, but it's the best, most useful thing you can learn. I'll admit that I haven't always been the very best listener in the past – *especially* if some of my old teachers are reading – but if you concentrate on what people are telling you, you can learn from much more than just their words. For example, if I listen to Phil and Holly interviewing someone who is a bit nervous, I'm not just learning about what the nervous person thinks. I'm hearing all of the clever tips and techniques Phil and Holly use to put people at their ease.

Remember that you don't need to meet someone to be inspired by them

This might be the most important one. You don't need a phone book full of celebrities. You don't need to be taught by a top academic at a big university. You don't need an audience with Oprah (although you must never pass this up, if you have the opportunity). You could spend your life locked in a cupboard and, as long as you had a phone and Wi-Fi access, you could spend hours with some of the most inspiring people in the universe by simply binge-watching TED talks. Listen to the radio and hear passionate, talented speakers discuss the things that matter most to them. Watch *Dumbo* and think about how you might use your biggest insecurity and turn it into a superpower. Also, you don't necessarily need someone to mentor you and inspire you to become one of the greatest philosophers of our age. Start small, fire up YouTube and find a mentor who can show you the best way to use a blow-dryer. Whether you're making improvements inside your head or on your head, it all counts.

Age is nothing but a number

As you know, I adore spending time with older people, and their wisdom is well documented. It stands to reason that anyone who has been on Earth for longer than you will know more than you do, and they'll be a great mentor. However, I've learned not to discount people who are my own age, or people who are younger than me. It's much easier to find inspiring people if you're prepared to find something inspiring in everyone. Admittedly, most of the people I'm inspired by are a bit older than me, because I'm only twenty-three. The only way I'll meet younger people is if I start hanging out in sand-pits. Still, there might be something to be said for that. I'm definitely inspired by the way that babies are so good at living in the moment. They're not constantly messing around with their phones or worrying about FOMO. Also, they always look way better in a onesie than anyone else. Seriously, though, when people started to tell me that I was

> It's much easier to find inspiring people if you're prepared to find something inspiring in everyone.

helping them because of the way I spoke about my skin when it was bad, it hit me that you don't need to feel like a grown-up to inspire people. If I was able to motivate them, I could definitely be inspired by anyone – not just people I meet inside Churchill's War Rooms.

Turn jealousy into positivity

Is there someone in your life that you envy so badly that you sometimes think of them at four in the morning, when you can't sleep, and hiss, audibly? Do you have a friend whose Instagram posts force you to hurl your phone across the room, because you want their life so badly? Have you ever cried in the loo after hearing about someone else's promotion? Well, stop sobbing and start celebrating, because you've just found yourself a surprise mentor!

I'll admit that I've not experienced much jealousy in my life, and I don't have a very envious nature, but I am aware that we're all living at a time when it's hard not to feel the odd awkward, resentful pang. When everyone is constantly documenting the best bits of their lives, we can feel as though it's a real struggle to keep up. For me, the jealousy usually hits when I see a party on social media that I'm not at. For some of my friends, it's a combination of new clothes, holidays and career goals. The funny thing about jealousy is that it usually has something to tell us. If you want your life to be more like someone else's, that envy can be inspiring, and that person you envy might have some very useful things to teach you. More to the point, if they're showing you their life on social media, they're sharing useful, inspiring information.

Next time someone makes you jealous, don't resist the feeling. Lean into it. Tell them, nicely. Say, 'I'd love to do that! Can you tell me how you did it?' Do try to avoid the words *damn you* and *bitch*. If you engage with the person you're jealous of, you'll get a much better, broader picture of what their life is like, and the amount of hard work and organization that goes into achieving it. You might discover some brand-new passions, and hopefully you'll make a new friend.

Be bold – ask!

When you admire someone, asking them to help you can be terrifying. It's easy to assume that they're going to be far too grand and important to bother with you. However, asking for help is the best thing you can do. It's hugely flattering, and it doesn't matter how important someone is – they'll be thrilled if they think they've inspired you in some way. Even if they say no, they'll be nice about it, but there's a good chance that they'll make a big effort to help, because they want to pay it forward. Mentors don't come out of nowhere; they only exist because other people have helped, supported and advised them. They know that, if they give you a hand, one day you'll be able to help someone else.

When you're approaching a potential mentor, the best thing to do is to be very specific. Don't just say that you want to be

> ❝ When I listen to Phil and Holly interviewing someone who is a bit nervous, I'm not just learning about what the nervous person thinks. I'm hearing all of the clever tips and techniques they use to put people at their ease. ❞

like them. Focus on a specific aspect of their work or career that interests you and ask for details. This shows that you're interested and committed enough to benefit from their expertise, and it also ensures you'll get a proper answer from them. 'Can you give me some career advice?' is a very difficult question for anyone to answer, and it usually comes back to not getting drunk and photocopying your bum. (Although, if you were asking me, I'd probably tell you to go for it.)

The best advice I've been given by others

It's very hard to give anyone helpful, sensible advice without knowing their situation, but these are some of the best, most useful bits of information I've learned about getting the most out of life. Even though I'm young, I've had so many exciting opportunities, and following these rules has helped me to embrace every single chance that has come my way, as well as leading me to the next one.

'Dress well, because you never know who you're going to meet'
Granny Denise

My granny has such high style standards that you'd never see her popping out for a pint of milk in her pyjamas. This is partly because she's too organized to run out of milk, but also because she believes that, if you're dressed well, you're prepared for anything. If you see Prince Harry or Zayn Malik in Tesco Metro, you want to feel confident enough to go over and say hello. It's easier to do this in beautifully laundered separates than it is in fleecy sleepwear with toothpaste stains on the knees.

'It doesn't matter what you achieve, as long as you work hard for it'
Mum

My mum is a big believer in potential, and she hates to see it wasted. In her world, having any ability and not working hard is like accumulating hundreds of pounds of Boots Advantage points and then leaving your card and all of your shopping on the bus. Mum has shown me that the work should be as exciting as the reward, and it's the effort that makes something worth having. Because of her, I'm inspired to pick the work I find really challenging.

'Get an early night'
Gemma, my manager

Poor Gemma! I'm suggesting that she's some sort of recluse who is against going out, but actually she's the one who reminds me that sleep isn't a chore, but a basic biological need that humans can't function without. Gemma has shown me that getting to bed early might seem boring, but it leads to brilliant things, and that it's always worth resting and preparing properly, rather than trying to wing it with a hangover. Also, it's much more fun to go out as a reward, once you've survived your early start and aced all of your tasks because you've got a good night's sleep behind you.

'Make sure your date brings you to your door'
Stanley Johnson

While Stanley is definitely a contemporary thinker – he's even starting to embrace Snapchat – he's awfully old-fashioned when it comes to dating and matters of the heart. Specifically, he's told me that, even though equal opportunities are important, if someone takes me out, they have to treat me like a lady and make sure that I get home safely. Stanley is a big believer in respect, and he's inspired me to raise my romantic standards. Before, boys didn't always treat me well, and I'd sometimes let it slide instead of making a fuss. However, Stanley has shown me to look for signs of respect, and, if there don't appear to be many, there is no second date.

'Do your squats. Eat your vegetables. Wear red lipstick. And don't let boys be mean to you'
Kendall Jenner

I couldn't resist including some advice from a Kardashian, because I think they might be some of the most confident creatures of the age we live in! When I've visited LA, I've been surrounded by people who seem to live by this mantra. It's extremely American, but pretty effective, and while I never actually want to do my squats, I always feel a bit better afterwards. Mind you, quite a lot of people in California seem to *drink* their vegetables, and I have mixed feelings about liquidized kale. Still, we should never let men be mean to us, and I suspect a spirulina smoothie is the perfect punishment for badly-behaved boys.

What Next?

As you know, I'm incredibly ambitious, and even though I'm extremely proud of what I've achieved, I'm really just getting started. I'm so excited about all the opportunities that lie ahead, and hopefully I'll be working for *ages* yet. I'm not sure what life will have thrown at me by the time I'm thirty, but I have so many dreams and goals. Here's what I'm hoping will happen.

One of the best things to come out of my time in the jungle was the chance to write a column in the *Sunday Times*. I loved it, and it made me realize that I want to write more in the future. Because I've always been the sort of girl who leaves her homework until the very last minute, I thrive on tight deadlines, and I found myself making notes and working on it all week long. Because I'm rarely in one place for long, I constantly write anecdotes and funny stories on my phone, or in a notebook I keep with me. One of my favourite things is my fountain pen, and I love writing in ink, but it's not always the most practical thing to take on a night out, especially if you're eating dinner on a white tablecloth! I think my love of writing is linked to my passion for current affairs. Journalism is a real love of mine, and I hope to do much more of it, especially if it gives me the chance to grill some more politicians! Researching topics to write about makes me very happy, and I get intensely nerdy about it.

As well as writing, I've fallen in love with broadcast journalism, and I'm really hoping that I can do more live T.V.! So far, most of the work I've done has been on the lighter side, and I always have so much fun working on the funnier items. It feels very natural. Still, I really enjoy the work when it has a more serious side, too. Working on the piece about my skin for *This Morning* is one of the things I'm the most proud of. I also felt so grateful to have the opportunity to work on an item about sustainability on *Watchdog*. It's something I'm becoming increasingly aware of, and I know that I have a platform I can use to make a difference.

My generation is really environmentally conscious, and we all want to know what we can do in order to make a difference. I hope that, over the coming years, I'll be involved in some environmental campaigns and will find a way of talking about the issues that makes them relatable. After all, I'm not an expert, but I've become really aware of waste since I started living on my own, and I think that most of us want to know how we can treat the environment well, in a way that genuinely makes the difference.

Being in the jungle put this in perspective for me, too. It made me really aware of nature, in a way that I wasn't before. I'm so keen to make sure that I can inspire people and make a difference, as well as making people laugh.

Of course, my big passion is politics, but I'm not sure I could ever see myself as PM, or even Chief Whip! For me, politics is a hobby. I can talk about it endlessly, but I wish I could find a way of being more involved, without necessarily being attached to a political party. My big dream is to get more young people registered to vote, and I'd love for the voting age to be lowered to sixteen; I'd much rather campaign for that than tell people how to vote. Maybe one day I could stand as an independent candidate, and my slogan would be, *I don't care who you vote for – I just care that you vote!* It would be amazing if I could combine politics with T.V. work. I think my big dream would be to make a documentary or series about getting more young people involved in the political process.

> ❝ I know that the worst thing I could do is forget where I came from, and I need my family to remind me. ❞

Another part of my job that I'm really enjoying and hoping to do more of is the brand work. I've always been really open about the fact that I enjoy using Instagram in a commercial way. I'm an influencer, I need content, and I'm always really happy to endorse a brand when I'd wear their clothes anyway. I think it works for me because I love fashion and I adore putting outfits together.

However, I've been offered lots of money to endorse brands I'm not fond of, and I always say no. I've bought from online stores before where I've worn their dress once, and then watched it fall apart in the washing machine. If I wouldn't wear something because it wasn't good quality, there's no way that I could tell anyone else to. (For starters, Granny Denise would be furious with me!)

I do get lots of lovely comments about my clothes, and I really hope that this allows me to do more work with fashion as I get older. My dream would be to do a long-term collaboration with a brand, and really curate a collection, as my personal style evolves all the time. Well, my true dream would be to get a call from Karl Lagerfeld, demanding my input as a creative director and muse. But I'm probably a bit too busy at the moment – so, Karl, if you're reading this, call me in six months!

Toff's top ten ultimate survival tips

1. Always pack a snack

Nothing in the world is worse than being 'hangry'. Most of my friends thought that I'd be the first to get voted out of the jungle, because I get so grumpy and filled with rage if I haven't eaten enough! Weeks of witchetty grubs have made me feel so grateful for the fact that I'm usually always within a few metres of a Mars Bar. I've seen *The Devil Wears Prada* and I'm sure that's why everyone in that film was supposed to be so terrifying – for the sake of fashion, they weren't eating! Whether you're out dancing, you've got a long afternoon in the office, or you're worried about getting stuck in a traffic jam, *bring something to eat*. It will keep your blood sugar up and the hanger at bay. Life is too short to skip snacks.

2. Don't let boys hold you back

Before going into the jungle, I made the decision to break up with my boyfriend, just because I *knew* that I'd be horribly distracted if I was worrying about what he was getting up to while I was in Australia. I think this is the best decision I ever made, because it let me really throw myself into every task and make the most of every moment. I'm sure there's no way I could have won if I'd been lovesick and mopey, but, more importantly, I had the experience of a lifetime, and I would have missed out if I'd put my love life first. There will be a time in my life when I have to balance work with a partner and family. Still, right now, I'm young and I feel as though everything is ahead of me. I've decided that dating is not my priority, and my career is the thing that I care about the most. As a result, work is going brilliantly and I'm really happy.

3. Find the funny in every situation

I've said it before, and I'll say it again: ultimately, everything is hilarious. I think I've always liked to see the funny side, and being in the jungle really brought home to me how important this is. When everyone is starving, homesick and the nearest proper loo is over an hour away, it's easy to let the darkness take over, and think you might be living in a tragedy. For the sake of survival, it's vital to see the comedy in wiping your bum on a load of leaves or having to crawl through a tank of lizards just to get some dinner. It was very funny. We'd all chosen to be there, voluntarily, and if that doesn't make you laugh during the difficult times, nothing will. I think it helped that I'd had so much practice in laughing through life's obstacles, like being pied off by boys, and walking down the King's Road with my skirt tucked into my knickers.

4. Don't whinge, and don't let anyone else get away with it

Admittedly, we all need to let off steam sometimes, and if you've just had a parking ticket, or the pub has run out of crisps, it's very difficult to shrug and pretend it doesn't matter. Still, moaning is dangerously addictive, and once you start complaining, you start to see everything in an extremely negative light. It makes you sad, and it brings down everyone around you. I'm not a natural whinger, so if someone says something negative, I'm the positive Pollyanna who counteracts it with something cheerier. ('Well, we could try a mix of peanuts and pork scratchings!' I'm sure it gets quite irritating at times.)

I think whinging is ruder and more unpleasant than farting in public, to be honest. At least farts can be extremely funny, and they're forgotten as soon as you open a window. Whinging really poisons the atmosphere, as everyone competes to be grumpier and gloomier.

On difficult days in the jungle, everyone could get really negative, really quickly. I understood that it was extremely hard, especially for the people who were missing their families. Still, I knew that whinging would make everything worse, so I tried to stay as positive as possible in order to distract people and remind everyone to have a bit of perspective on what was going on.

If you can resist the urge to whinge, and interrupt the flow of the complainers, you'll start to build up a mental muscle that helps you to see something good in every situation.

5. Be brave, even when it's very difficult

I was going to tell you that my beloved Churchill said, 'The only thing we have to fear is fear itself,' but luckily I googled it first and discovered that it actually came from Franklin D. Roosevelt during his 1932 election campaign. Still, it's a great, useful quote, because it reminds us that nothing is ever as horrifying as it seems in our imagination – and that's what being brave is all about. From the moment I jumped on the zip wire, on the way to the *I'm A Celebrity* camp, I knew that I was about to take on a series of the scariest challenges I'd ever faced. Yet, the scary part is mental, not physical, and once I realized this, I was able to fully throw myself into everything.

Generally, the rule is that you can spend hours, days and weeks *dreading* the thing that you need to be brave for, but the thing itself will usually last a few minutes at most. You might not have to go on a zip wire that's several thousand feet above ground level, but you might have to take an exam, ask someone out or go to a job interview. Remember that it can't possibly be as scary as it seems in your head, and also, that it will all be over quite quickly. You'll be fine. The more time you spend being brave, the easier it becomes, and you'll get so good that you'll spend all of your weekends at zoos, sticking your head into tigers' mouths for a laugh. (Please, don't do this.)

6. Embrace your inner Jungle Barbie

Way back, long ago, in lion times, the spirit of Mufasa descended from the sky to tell Simba, 'Remember who you are!' Well, you don't have to be a fan of *The Lion King* to find this advice useful. When I went into the jungle, I was worried that everyone would write me off and think I was a bimbo. I had two choices. I could have done my very best Lara Croft impression and spent weeks pretending to be someone else. (If I'm honest, I would have got caught out *straight* away, because, if I'm in a stressful situation, I get archaeology mixed up with architecture, and if someone asked a question about a tomb of the pharaoh, I'd think they were talking about a delicious ball-shaped chocolate covered in hazelnuts.) Or, I could have thought, *You know what? I am a bit of a bimbo, and that's really why I'm here. If they'd wanted Bear Grylls, they would have phoned his agent. They wanted someone who can navigate the third floor of Selfridges, not a swamp.*

❛ My true dream would be to get a call from Karl Lagerfeld, demanding my input as a creative director and muse. But I'm probably a bit busy at the moment – call me in six months, Karl! ❜

So, I decided there was no point in trying to be anyone but me. This is what I've learned from working in reality T.V. for so long. It's very hard to be fake, because everything you do is captured and caught, and you can't hide the truth. All I could do was turn up and be the most authentic version of myself – the one who thinks that a snake pit is a club near Earl's Court that used to do £1 shots.

Being Jungle Barbie had some surprising advantages. People were expecting me to be a little bit feeble, but I shocked them by showing them how tough I could be. To be honest, I shocked myself! Still, I think the best part of it was the fact that I felt so happy and relaxed, because I'd made a decision to show my personality in its full girly glory.

You don't have to be Jungle Barbie, but you might be surprised by how good it feels to identify the most mockable part of your personality and make it your personal brand! Being able to laugh at yourself is an essential survival skill. We waste so much time worrying about being embarrassed and wondering what might go wrong if we let ourselves be vulnerable. Lean into who you are, even the weirdest, strangest, silliest parts. You'll learn that, when you don't try to hide any part of your personality, nothing can hold you back.

7. Be consistent – if you'd say it behind someone's back, be prepared to say it to their face

Again, reality T.V. has trained me very well by showing me that all of our behaviour has consequences, and if you're running around causing trouble and saying different things to different people, your entire life will blow up in your face in about three seconds.

Sometimes, conflict is unavoidable, and if someone has done something to hurt or offend you, you're well within your rights to be a bit bitchy. This is as long as you can imagine yourself in a situation where they might stride up to you in the middle of a Roaring Twenties themed party and confront you with your own words, while trying not to stab their own eyes out with a feathered headdress. Can you deal with this, and keep a straight face? If the answer is no, it's best to stay silent.

I think that the bitching and tension in the jungle was very different, partly because the situation was much more extreme. I'm sure that everyone said and did the odd thing they now regret, but I'm also sure that nothing negative would have come up if everyone had had access to hot baths and buttered toast. Luckily, my experiences in Chelsea had taught me everything I needed to know about handling the situation. I'd been to Mean Girl (and Boy) 101, and I knew that bitching comes with serious risks attached.

The rule is quite simple, really. If you're cross with someone and end up falling out with them, it's probably better to be honest about your feelings, even though it will be difficult and painful for both of you. If they know you've told the truth, you might be able to recover the friendship further down the line. However, if you've been bitching about them and you get caught out lying about it, they won't be able to trust you, because they'll think you're mean *and* a liar. Sometimes, life is easier if you follow the old rule: if you can't say anything nice, don't say anything at all, and certainly not on camera!

8. Put family first

At the moment, I don't have much free time, so, whenever I have a day off, I call my mum and try to do something with her. Sometimes, I think I have a family battery. When we've not spent a lot of time together for a few weeks, my energy levels start running really low, and I know that I need to go back home and charge up. It's really important to spend time with people who know you well, and don't need you to act a certain way in order to entertain them. The thing I love the most about being with my mum is that I can just *be*, and I'm allowed to relax properly.

Family means something different to everyone, but, for me, it's about finding the people who love me exactly as I am, and don't expect anything from me. They are the ones who let me make stupid jokes that would make no sense to anyone else. The people I don't have to bother wearing mascara for. The people whose doorbell I can ring while standing outside in my pyjamas and Ugg boots. I know I'm incredibly fortunate to be so close to my family, and to have friends who make me feel as though I'm part of their family.

I think that many of us will find all kinds of different families during our twenties and beyond, but we might also struggle to remember that these relationships are really important. At the moment, I'm truly having the time of my life. In the last year or so, I've had more incredible experiences and opportunities than

I thought I'd experience in a lifetime, and I've had the chance to travel all over the world and meet my idols. Still, I know that the worst thing I could do is forget where I came from, and I need my family to remind me. This is why I have to make them my priority. I really hope that I'm working and having adventures for a long time, but my family will be in my life forever, and I can't take them for granted. To put it simply, the most effective survival skill I know is calling my mum. It always works.

9. Cleanse your phone

Our phones are full of rubbish, aren't they? Firstly, we take them everywhere, and I shudder to think about how unhygienic it is to constantly touch something, especially if you've ever played Candy Crush on the loo. Still, it's not just a practical issue, but an emotional one. If your phone is full of exes' numbers, or you have seventeen meditation apps you don't use, which you downloaded during an extreme period of stress, or you keep thousands of photos of the last night out you went on with a former friend, you're carrying around a constant reminder of your saddest, most difficult times. We all do it, especially because we use our phones for absolutely everything, and we're not going to buy brand-new ones simply to celebrate being newly single – not when transferring everything over is such a nightmare.

It can be hugely liberating to go on a big deleting spree. If it feels a bit daunting, try putting the bad apps in a faraway folder, so that nothing is gone forever – but it's out of sight, out of mind. My biggest break-up haunted me for a long time, until I did the unthinkable and removed all evidence from my phone forever. It made it much easier for me to move on. Deliveroo, you know my feelings for you were too intense for love to last, but I will never forget those bacon sandwiches we enjoyed together. Now, I'm in a happier, healthier place, and I can't keep you on my phone, reminding me of the good times. Maybe, one day, we can be friends.

10. When in doubt, plan a party

If you want to survive and thrive, you need to fill your life with things to look forward to, and there's nothing more cheering than the prospect of a jolly good dance. During the toughest moments in Australia, I'd spur myself on by dreaming about the massive night out my friends might plan for me as soon as I got back. In fact, that's the only way I could deal with the pythons. My body might have been at the snake trial, but my heart and soul were with my pals, boogying to some serious cheese at 151.

I suspect that most of us don't have enough parties, and I'd love to see that changing. When the world is filled with things to worry about, we need parties more than ever. We will never lie on our deathbeds, look back at our lives and wish we'd had *less* champagne. Parties don't need to be grand, either. You just need two or more people, a few bottles of Blossom Hill and a speaker. Maybe pizza, if you want to push the boat out. I love a themed party, and I don't think a theme can ever be too specific. 'Diamonds, dresses and drama' is a great theme, but so is, 'I've failed my driving test for the third time and I just bought a bottle of vodka.' Ultimately, parties are only ever as good as the people you invite to them, so party planning is an excellent survival tool, as it's a way of drawing your favourite people close to you and bonding with them.

So, this feels like a good place to leave you, dreaming of parties and being surrounded by all your favourite people. When I started writing this book, I wondered how much advice I really had to give; I'm only twenty-three, after all. But one of the best things I learned when I was in the jungle was that no one really knows very much about anything. Everyone gets scared, everyone gets anxious, and there isn't a single one of us that can prepare for all of the situations life might throw at us. We never know how strong we are until we need to use our strength. Your Bushtucker Trials might be metaphorical and involve problems at work or fights with your family, but you'll need to use the same skills that I used when I faced a less than tasty insect dinner. This time last year, I didn't know that I was capable of handling something so challenging, but I'm sure that you can deal with things that are just as difficult. I *can* tell you how to do it with a smile on your face. Being positive takes practice, but life is, essentially, hilarious.

Acknowledgements

Being given the opportunity to write this book was such an exciting opportunity for me, it has been a joy. My time in the jungle made me think so much about a particular group of people, my family. You make me both cry with laughter and my heart burst with love. Mum, Dad thank you for everything you've given me, the love and nurture is something I hope I pass on to my children one day. I also want to thank my grandparents for everything you've done for me, the relationship I have with both of you is so special. Sometimes I sit and pinch myself for being so blessed with you two.

This brings me on to my aunties, uncles and cousins. Thank you for your generosity, love and laughter over the past twenty-three years. I adore you all. Everything I am I owe to you crazy lot. For that I thank you.

Lastly - thank you to my editor Jane Sturrock for your faith in me! We did it! Thanks, too, to the hardworking team at Quercus I couldn't have done it without every single one of you. I reserve the most enormous thanks for Daisy Buchanan for being such a good listener and now an even better friend.

How do you stay positive and keep smiling? Toff's fans share their best tips!

"I look at my daughter and think of the happiness she's brought into my life and the little lady she's become (she's 7) and the life she will live in the future. p.s. she loves you Toff!"

@charlotteandreese

"Sunflowers! I love sunflowers. They remind me to always be bright, stand tall and to spread a little sunshine wherever I go!"

@helloooro

"I play music, very badly but I pick up my guitar (or ukulele or sit at the piano) grab a mic and annoy my family until I've chilled out a bit. Singing out the stress"

@_alice_gordon_

"Find 3 things that went well each day and focus on those (rather that focusing on things that didn't go to plan) x"

@rachelroedel

"Working with children (aged 3-5) each day knowing I have made an impact on their little lives just by making them laugh, playing with them, answering all their random questions. Best feeling to be shaping little hearts and life's #AlwaysSmiling"

@daniellsteel8

"Fluffy socks, warm blanket and a book whilst sitting in front of an open window always makes me feel more connected with myself and more positive!"

@michavidot

"I write a blog – Not necessarily for other people to read, but so I can document happy things in my life. Also, when things aren't great, it helps me to look at it differently and see the good, because when I write it down and think, it helps me put things into perspective. If one person reads it and feels inspired by it, that's enough xxx"

@bellat66

"I like to live by the phrase 'choose your attitude' . . . decide that nothing can bring you down and that giving out a positive vibe will help build other people up"

@kazeebeth

"Other than hearing your positive vibes, I love to cycle, run, spending time with my husband planning our future trips, this guarantees putting a smile on my face . . . oh and my guilty pleasure watching #Topgear & #MIC"

@sam_doubleh_g

"I pick my 6-year-old nephew up from school. We go home and play the doughnut game. You have to eat a doughnut without licking your lips. This creates hysteria. He has 2 of the most perfect dimples and when he laughs my heart melts. It's always the simple things that keep you smiling"

@dancrow72

"Grab each day by the horns and enjoy it like it was your last. Fill it with smiles, kind gestures, excitement and with people who make you feel good. Reach the end of each day and think about the good moments to paste over any that could possibly get you down. If that fails, get in your car, put on some tunes and sing as loud as you can. As soon as people start staring, sing at them and you'll both probably end up smiling. Haha"

@couzensallin

"Singing along to Robbie Williams 'I love my life' track in the car with the volume turned up"

@saraharris

Meditation – particularly outside in green grass with the sun on my face"

@jessicaantonialydia

"I love cooking, especially baking, as it is very therapeutic. The smell of freshly baked goodies puts a smile on everybody's face. Also if you have had a hard day at work, when kneading your dough you can expel negative energy by pound the hell out of it. And it makes me happy to see people eating and enjoying my food. I also like to do meditation as it helps me relax."

@cararuggeri

"I travel as much as I can, either abroad or just playing tourist in my hometown! Stepping out of everyday life, even just for a weekend, is a beautiful reminder of everything good that the world has to offer and all the positive things you have back home"

@shannsberry

"I go to as many music-oriented things as I can throughout the year. Music makes me happy and life is about having fun. Everyone smiles when there is music being played xx"

@riola_81

"Believe it or not, my job makes me happy. I work in a nursery and when you're sad, or anything outside of work gets you stressed, you forget all of that when the children smile at you. It's infectious!! Children don't realise it but they are truly magic! They give you cuddles, draw you pictures, do silly things that make you laugh and you forget about all the things that got you down before you got to work. I'm truly grateful to have picked this for a career and happy to have all my little friends at my job"

@lozpot123

"When I'm feeling sad I like to get my family together and have one big roast dinner, eat my feelings and realise everything is okay after some roast beef and Yorkshire puddings"

@brookeegeorgiaa

"I love to bake! Cakes, cupcakes, bread, whatever it is, I love baking food and sharing it with my friends and family. It takes my mind off things and makes me grin like a Cheshire cat after its finished and ready to eat!!!"

@fawjiayasmin

"Every year a few of us dads meet up and take our kids camping and just do really cool stuff that the kids would enjoy doing all weekend, like a adventure trek or even just catching crabs at the seaside or exploring some woods. Seeing what we can find makes me smile when I look back at what we have done"

@richardmanson1975

"I am always referred to as the positive one and your post made me think 'what do I do to stay so positive?'. Then I realised I eat a well-balanced and filling breakfast. If I'm set up for the day from the beginning then literally nothing can bring me down!"

@ginakezza

"I ask myself, is there anything that you can do about it ? If there is . . . do it . . . if there isn't . . . try not to stress about things I cannot control ! Failing that a good ole rant to my mum followed by some therapeutic colouring does the trick"

@laura.398

"I keep a good circle of people around me, I run from Notting Hill to Richmond and back and I talk everything out with my Dad x"

@marcalexwatts

"I found that the main reason of me being unhappy was due to what I expected of others, either the way they act or maybe they were meant to do something! so LETTING GO OF EXPECTATIONS is what I do to keep myself happy! Not everything will go the way we want it to in life and that's okay. I think we need to stop putting our happiness in someone else's hands and make ourselves happy! And if that fails . . . well there's always wine!"

@justahappyginger

"I create a very long to-do list, which details all the little things that I think are causing me to be worried or stressed! Once it's all layed out on paper with easy steps to accomplish each, I feel so much better & can get on with my day"

@justkatiepa